"It is no longer a question of whether or not we should set aside some more of the yet remaining native California landscape as 'breathing space'...if we do not, we will leave our children a legacy of concrete treadmills leading nowhere except to other congested places like those they will be trying to get away from."

—Former Congressman Clem Miller
Author of legislation to create
Point Reyes National Seashore

EXPLORING POINT REYES

by Phil Arnot & Elvira Monroe

A Guide to Point Reyes National Seashore

REVISED EDITION

Wide World Publishing/Tetra

cover photograph: Phil Arnot on the hills at Kehoe Beach.
interior photographs by Phil Arnot

Wide World Publishing/Tetra
P.O. Box 476
San Carlos, CA 94070

Printed in the United States of America

First printing 1976
Sixth Edition 1994

ISBN: 0-884550-00-2

Library of Congress Cataloging-in-Publication Data

Arnot, Phil.
    Exploring Point Reyes.

    Includes index.
    1. Hiking—California—Point Reyes National Seashore—
Guide Books. 2. Backpacking—California—Point Reyes National
Seashore—Guide-books. 3. Trails—California—Point Reyes Na-
tional Seashore—Guide-books. 4. Point Reyes Natonal Seashore
(Calif.) I. Monroe, Elvira. II. Title.
GV199.42.C22P643 1989   917.94'62   89–5783
ISBN 1-884550-00-2

————————— ACKNOWLEDGMENTS —————————

We would like to express appreciation to the following:

John Sansing
Superintendent
Point Reyes National Seashore
for his encouragement, his referrals to resource material and his
introductory remarks.

The Rangers
at the Visitor Center, who patiently provided us with information.

And most especially to—

Harry Carpenter
Trails Foreman

John Dell'Osso
Park Ranger

Mia Monroe
Park Ranger

Steve Wolfe
Park Ranger

for their research, assistance with technical data and general related
information, and provision of resource materials.

Bass Lake viewed from the Coast Trail.

Greetings!.

On behalf of Point Reyes National Seashore, we would like to welcome you to this wonderful natural and cultural resource!

Point Reyes National Seashore, although within an hour's drive from a major urban area, contains some of the finest recreational and wilderness areas California has to offer. Dramatic coastal beaches and bluffs, life-filled saltwater marshes, towering quiet forests, and miles of wilderness trails are all available for your exploration.

The presence of places like Point Reyes, with its open spaces, abundant wildlife and rich coastline, remind us of the need to protect our natural resources.

We at the Park are dedicated to the preservation of our natural heritage and hope you will join us in supporting our efforts in the National Parks.

Whether you're looking for a quiet place to picnic or a vantage point to watch frolicking sea lions, I think you'll find it at Point Reyes. It has something for almost everyone; it's a special place by any standard.

Enjoy your visit!

> **John Sansing, Superintendent**
> **Point Reyes National Seashore**
> **Point Reyes Station, CA 94956**

Arch Rock Overlook—looking south toward Double Point.

───────── TABLE OF CONTENTS ─────────

Double Point along Wildcat Beach

HOW TO GET TO POINT REYES NATIONAL SEASHORE

To get to Point Reyes National Seashore Visitor Center (Olema), under normal traffic conditions from any of the following locations, allow time as indicated. The time estimates offered here are based on the assumption that you drive on or about the speed limit.

Berkeley (via San Rafael-Richmond Bridge)	1 hr 15 min
Oakland (via San Rafael-Richmond Bridge)	1 hr 30 min
Walnut Creek (via San Rafael-Richmond Bridge)	1 hr 50 min
San Francisco (via Golden Gate Bridge)	1 hr 15 min
San Mateo (via Golden Gate Bridge)	1 hr 35 min
Redwood City (via Golden Gate Bridge)	1 hr 45 min
Palo Alto (via Golden Gate Bridge)	1 hr 50 min
San Rafael	45 min
Mill Valley	50 min
Terra Linda	50 min
Sausalito	55 min

If you plan to start from a trailhead more distant than the one at the Visitor Center, add the following number of minutes to the time chart above:

Estero Trailhead	20-25 min
Muddy Hollow Trailhead	20 min
Limantour Trailhead	20 min
Five Brooks Trailhead	10 min
Abbotts Lagoon Trailhead	20-25 min
Kehoe Beach Trailhead	25-30 min
McClures Beach Trailhead	35-40 min
Palomarin Trailhead	40-45 min

Once in Marin county and heading for the National Seashore, I suggest you avoid State Highway 1 from where it leaves Highway 101 near Sausalito to Point Reyes National Seashore. Instead, take Sir Francis Drake Highway, which junctions with Highway 101 at Greenbrae. If time is not a consideration, Highway 1 is very scenic. On a highway map Highway 1 appears more direct, but the highway maps don't show the many narrow winding curves. Traveling from the Bear Valley Trailhead to either Palomarin Trailhead or Five Brooks Trailhead, do take the highway *from its junction with the Sir Francis Drake Highway at Olema only.* In this stretch Highway 1 is direct, as well as scenic. Heading south for Palomarin Trailhead from the Bear Valley Trailhead, turn off Highway 1 towards Bolinas, and turn right on Mesa Road, just outside Bolinas. Mesa Road winds for 4-5 miles before reaching Palomarin trailhead.

On Sunday afternoons in spring, summer, fall, and sometimes even in winter, the southbound traffic on the Golden Gate Bridge gets backed up bumper to bumper almost as far as the Waldo tunnel from around 3:30 p.m. until 6 or 7 p.m. Take your time hiking and do not plan to reach your car until about 5 or 6 p.m. Explore having dinner in Olema or in Point Reyes Station. This will put you behind the traffic.

PUBLIC TRANSPORTATION

Since transportation company schedules change from year to year it is best to call the Point Reyes National Seashore Visitor Center (415)663-1092 for the latest information. At this writing, The Golden Gate Transit Company has very limited bus service to Point Reyes National Seashore.

The meadow at the junction of the Sky Trail and the Woodward Valley Trail.

On going efforts are being made to include *disabled visitors* to all buildings and programs. A copy of the Point Reyes accessibility guide is free of charge from any of the Park's visitor centers. The National Park Service provides a wheelchair for temporary use by park visitors. No rental fee is charged. The wheelchair is available at the Bear Valley Visitor Center.

CRITERIA FOR HIKING ROUTE CLASSIFICATION

Hikes in Point Reyes National Seashore have been classified as easy, moderate, or strenuous. The criteria for placing hikes in these categories is primarily distance, and secondarily change in elevation. Yet, the ultimate criteria for deciding which distances or elevation changes constitute an "easy" hike and which constitute a "strenuous" hike is subjective. After hiking 8 to 9 miles at a 3-3.5 miles an hour pace (allowing for occasional stops to examine flower, fauna, vistas, to take pictures, eat lunch) my knee and hip joints are not sore. After 18-25 miles at the same pace with the same allowance for breaks these joints do hurt.

CRITERIA

Easy Hike	4-9 miles
Moderate Hike	10-16 miles
Strenuous Hike	17-25 miles

If one climbs over 1500 feet on a given hike one can move the classification up a half or a full notch on the scale. There is no single climb of over 1400 feet at Point Reyes (any place on the beach to Mount Wittenberg), but one might select a route involving a number of different hill climbs which would total over 1500 feet of uphill hiking.

Actually, what is strenuous, moderate, or easy is relative to the individual. Each person must set his or her own classification system.

Heading west on Drakes Beach.

TABLE CONVERTING MILES TO KILOMETERS

Miles	Kilometers	Miles	Kilometers
1	1.6	10.5	16.8
1.5	2.4	11	17.6
2	3.2	11.5	18.4
2.5	4.0	12	19.2
3	4.8	12.5	20.0
3.5	5.6	13	20.8
4	6.4	13.5	21.6
4.5	7.2	14	22.4
5	8.0	14.5	23.2
5.5	8.8	15	24.0
6	9.6	15.5	24.8
6.5	10.4	16	25.6
7	11.2	16.5	26.4
7.5	12.0	17	27.2
8	12.8	17.5	28.0
8.5	13.6	18	28.8
9	14.4	18.5	29.6
9.5	15.2	19	30.4
10	16.0	19.5	31.2

Hikers on the Woodward Valley Trail.

CHAPTER 1

The Woodward Valley Loop

*Bear Valley Trailhead — Sky Trail —
Woodward Valley Trail — Coast Trail —
Bear Valley Trail — Bear Valley Trailhead.*

**12 miles
Moderately difficult**

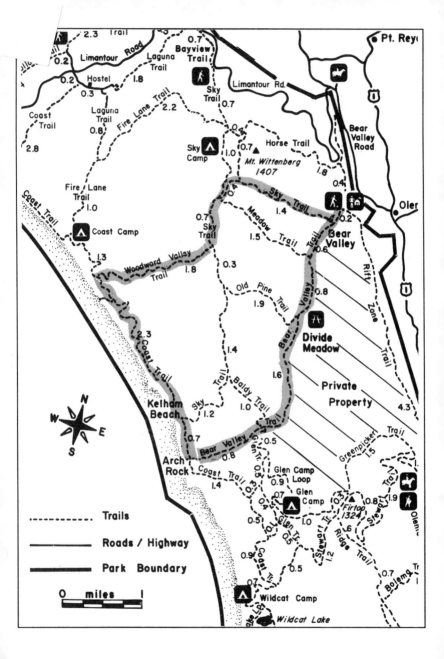

I f in a single day's 12 mile hike you want to experience sloping green meadows with lush undergrowth, rolling hills covered with wildflowers, an inspiring panorama of Drakes Bay and the Pacific Ocean beyond, open streams, waterfalls plunging over steep cliffs into the ocean, broad sandy beaches, sea caves and caverns, pelicans, seagulls, sea lions, woodpeckers, bluejays, hawks, brown deer, white deer, foxes, wildcats, chipmunks and, maybe, even a whale, then this hike is for you. In one spring day I experienced all of these things except a whale.

Try what I call the Woodward Valley Loop. You're guaranteed seeing all the land forms mentioned. Take the hike in spring and you'll have the greenery and flowers. As for the birds and animals, one can find them in any season. Only foxes, wildcats, and whales are less likely.

Setting out one spring day, I got a late start up the Sky Trail from its starting point some 200 yards from the Bear Valley Trailhead parking lot. It was two in the afternoon and the day was warm and sparkling. The Sky Trail begins to climb immediately, and I was soon sheltered from the sun by the groves of bay trees which arch across the trail. The warmth of the day brought out the pungent aroma of bay leaves.

In about a half mile I broke out onto an open meadow bordered by tall Douglas firs and gained my first view of Mount Wittenberg. The "mountain" is a high and open hill standing 1400' above sea level. From its open summit I would soon behold the expanse of Drakes Bay, sun spangles dancing on its surface on this rare windless spring afternoon. The trail led back into the forest only to emerge onto the green hillside some 400' below the top of Mount Wittenberg. At this point the Sky Trail is steepest and the hot sun and full pack caused rivers of perspiration to trickle down my body.

The trail skirts the summit of Mount Wittenberg and passes through another cluster of bay, oak, and fir trees leveling off on a broad open plateau immediately south of Mount Wittenberg. From the plateau, which was covered with lupine, poppies, and tidy tips, I took the short and steep (250') trail which leads from the sky trail to the summit.

I had covered the 1.5 mile climb much faster than I needed to, but my late start prompted me to hurry so as to miss as little of the midday as possible. The air was sweet with the aroma of the flowers. What looked like a canary (perhaps a yellow goldfinch or summer tanager) darted past my face headed for a coyote bush somewhere down the slope. Far to the southwest the Olema Valley stretched straight as the fault-line which runs through its length down towards Bolinas and Stinson Beach. Mount Tamalpais lay shimmering in the sunlight on the southeastern horizon. As my eyes scanned eastward, they touched the silhouette of Mount Diablo some 50 miles away. West and northwestward the ridges of Point Reyes peninsula, alternately wooded and open, plunged into the sea. Between the ridges, stream canyons covered with dense undergrowth moved towards Drakes Bay. As my eyes scanned the open plateau to the south they picked up something moving in the grass — one, then two, then three blacktail deer were grazing in the tall grass near a clump of small firs. They were but 100 yards off the Sky Trail which passes over the plateau.

I bounded down the slope of Mount Wittenberg back to the plateau and the Sky Trail in order to stalk the deer for some pictures and to resume my hike to the sea. Beyond the summit plateau the Sky

Trail, an old ranch road, dropped gradually to the densely wooded Inverness Ridge. Here the Sky Trail meets the Meadow Trail, coming up from Bear Valley, and enters the stately fir forest of the Inverness Ridge with its rich undergrowth of huckleberry, sword ferns, and other evergreen vegetation.

In about 3/4 mile I emerged from the forest into a small open meadow which stands at the head of Woodward Valley. I swung off the Sky Trail, which climbs southward and back into the forest, and turned westward onto the Woodward Valley Trail.

At this point Woodward Valley is a green amphitheater consisting of an elongated and slightly sunken lush green meadow flanked on three sides by dense dark green conifers and open at the western end. The trail moves parallel to the meadow towards the west and I was soon moving through it. Suddenly a black, red, and white woodpecker swooped gracefully above and across my path. I watched it sail on into the forest bordering the trail on the south.

Moving westward the trail began to descend slightly, then steeply, then to level off, and then to descend steeply again. Thus it followed an irregular but almost consistently declining attitude as it passed through forests, onto open hills, and back into the forest. At one point I emerged suddenly from the forest only to behold the brownish-white cliffs at Drakes Beach. These may have been the cliffs which reminded Drake of Dover when he landed somewhere in the Bay Area in 1579.

Suddenly the Woodward Valley Trail leveled off on an open ridge, then climbed, abruptly for 50' to a hilltop. 400 yards from the sea and some 500' above it, I found myself looking out upon the expanse of Drakes Bay all the way from Double Point 5 miles south to Point Reyes itself some 8 miles directly due west. The coastline formed a giant arc which contained the spangled waters of Drakes Bay. The Farallones Islands jutted up out of the sea on the western horizon. Alamere Falls plunged ribbon-like onto the sands of Wildcat Beach far to the south. On the landshelf below, the Coast Trail contoured at the base of the hills. On the hills themselves a cluster of white deer[1] grazed casually amidst clumps of grey-green coyote brush. Blue lilac gave off its sweet aroma along the trail which fell off steeply to its junction with the Coast Trail above Sculptured Beach.

Moving on, I followed the trail, as it descended over open hills for over 1/2 mile, to its junction with the Coast Trail, about a mile from Coast Camp. At the junction of the Coast Trail and the Woodward Valley Trail one has two options.

A left, or southeast, turn on the Coast Trail will take you along the broad coastal shelf above the sea to Miller point three miles from the junction and hence back to the Bear Valley Trailhead, via beautiful Bear Valley, 4.1 miles from Miller Point. This route is initially level and entirely open. It offers an expansive view of the sea including, on clear day, the Farallones Islands 30 miles away. And, in complete contrast, the last four miles on the Bear Valley Trail are characterized by deep woods and occasional meadows.

However, I took the second option by turning right towards Coast Camp 1.3 miles away on the Coast Trail. At Coast Camp I took the 100 yard access trail to the beach, turned left, and hiked 3/4 miles south to Sculptured Beach.

---

[1]Fallow Deer, native to Asia Minor and Mediterranean area of Europe. Obtained from San Francisco Zoo by a local rancher in 1947 and turned loose. Today's herd numbers a few hundred.

The northwest end of Sculptured Beach, which I came upon just after passing some tide pools next to Santa Maria creek, is marked by a small (9'—10') southeast facing cliff. This cliff is more of a problem to hikers coming opposite to my direction. They must climb it — unless they are able to pass around it at low tide — while I had only to jump down to the soft sands of Sculptured Beach. The climb isn't really dangerous, but it involves a 4 to 8 foot climb (depending on sand depth) on a broken 90 degree face.

Once on Sculptured Beach,[2] I moved 120 yards to a short cliff (7'), climbed to a shelf atop a small and rocky headland and, since the tide was low, dropped down to the beach on the other side of the small headland and made my way for perhaps 100 yards to a rocky archway through which I passed onto still another beach. The rocky archway was simply a hole in a second truncated headland similar to the one I had just climbed over. It is important to reemphasize that *this beach route should not be attempted except at low tide !*

On the section of beach to which the archway led, I had lunch in a sandy ampitheater surrounded on three sides by 200'–250' sheer walls of fluted soil and rock. Completing my lunch, I became sleepy and dozed off to the tune of gently lapping breakers and distant screeching of seagulls from somewhere down the beach.

I awakened with a start and with the feeling I was being watched. Sure enough. A pair of eyes, perched between a shiny bald head

---

[2]Be advised that the surf along Drakes Bay can be dangerous.

and a straw-like moustache, was searching me from less than 100 feet away. I was being studied by a sea lion. Suddenly another head popped up. And then another. All had probably come up from the rookery at Double Point 6 miles down the coast.[3]

I swung onto the beach again, engaged in a short conversation with the wary sea lions who ducked as I approached the shoreline. 300 yards southward I came upon the truncated headland which separates Sculptured Beach from Secret Beach. To reach Secret Beach I passed through an obvious "keyhole" in the truncated headland (safe passage only at minus low tides) to the northern end of Secret Beach. Passing through the keyhole I next needed to navigate some 30-40 feet of tidepools, before reaching the sands of Secret Beach. As soon as I set foot on sand I noticed, to my left, an enormous cave. Lowering my head, I passed under the entrance and into the interior of the cave. The cave was well known to me, for I always visit it when I'm on Secret Beach. Inside one finds a perfect miniature amphitheater surrounded by perpendicular walls leading upward to the top which is open to the sky. A perfect retreat — except at high tide!

Secret Beach is flanked by steep cliffs except for occasional creek canyons which knife through them presenting bushy escape routes

---

[3]During summer both *Stellar Sea Lions* and *California Sea Lions* may be seen. The *Stellar Sea Lion* bull weighs from 1500 to 2200 pounds and measures up to 13 feet. The female weighs about 600 pounds and be up to 9 feet. They are yellowish brown in color. The *California Sea Lion* bull weighs 500 to 900 pounds, and the female 200 to 600 pounds. Both measure 6 to 8 feet. Their color is dark brown or blackish. They are also distinguished by a ridge from the forehead to the rear of the skull called a sagittal crest.

The best place to see both kinds of Sea Lions is the Sea Lion Overlook, located 1/4 mile before the Point Reyes Lighthouse.

from the beach. Other creeks trickle over cliffs onto the sand creating, in one outstanding case, a perfect showerbath. One cannot continue southward on Secret Beach beyond the wall of Point Resistance which juts prominently out into the sea to divide Kelham Beach from Secret Beach. At the lowest of tides Point Resistance is sheer to the water. Traversing the cliff would be difficult and dangerous even with a rope. I therefore sought a way out by a cliff route with a 65-75 degree slope which *I would not recommend to anyone who has not done technical rock climbing* since the crumbly rock is 60' above the beach. Farther north, back from where I had come, two or three routes via short shallow cliffs or stream canyons can be found for those wishing to avoid exposed cliff climbing. *If you find yourself doing anything even closely resembling exposed cliff climbing, turn around, and select a safe route. Failing to find one, retrace your steps to Coast Camp or to Sculptured Beach and an access trail connecting the beach with the Coast Trail.*

My escape route up cliffs and along easy ledges brought me onto the broad shelf which stretches northwestward by southeastward above Drakes Bay and along the coast on which the Coast Trail meanders. Coming up to the trail from the edge of the cliff behind me, I could not see the trail until I came within six feet of it. It ran at right angles to me and was obscured by tall green grass.

Gliding southward along the Coast Trail, which I had left some 1 1.5 miles northward at its junction with Woodward Valley, I noticed more deer — this time in mixed groups of brown and white — grazing on the hills east and above the trail. I spent forty-five minutes stalking one group by crawling downwind behind them using coyote brush for a screen. I got close enough for a few telephoto pictures, but as I pressed closer the deer must have heard me. In an instant all heads lifted up and turned in my direction. For a moment they stood motionless in rapt attention. Then a white stag turned away and broke into a trot. The others turned almost as a unit and away they bounded up and through the coyote brush and out of sight. As I turned back to the trail, two wildcats swished through the grass not 50 yards away!

Farther south on the Coast Trail, which is open for its entire length, I reached the eucalyptus trees that mark the junction with the short trail to Kelham Beach.[4] In 300 steps I was on Kelham Beach at the point where Kelham Creek slithers down a rock face onto the beach. Drinking from the small waterfall[5] I turned and looked out on the sea to see the first of a squadron of pelicans slowly flapping northward, some 50'–70', above the breakers. A wind had come up by now and a second formation swooped down to glide just above the water and in the lee of a cresting breaker in order to gain shelter from the headwind.

Rather than return to the Coast Trail I decided to parallel it again and continue down the sandy stretches to Miller Point. There I would return to the Coast Trail by way of the Sea Tunnel. By now the tide was beginning to come in and I noticed whitecaps had erased the sun spangles. Sanderlings sprinted to and fro as they moved in and out with the breakers. 3/4 of a mile from Kelham Beach I encountered Coast Creek as it glides out from under the Sea Tunnel[6] onto the beach. Getting through the Sea Tunnel required

---

[4]Watch for poison oak along the sides of this trail.

[5]The National Park Service advises against drinking the water in the Seashore area. Water can be treated—one iodine purification tablet per quart of water. Let it dissolve for 20 minutes before drinking.

[6]At very high tides, or during storms, this should not be attempted. In the 26 years I had known the Sea Tunnel there had been a single tunnel but in April 1986 the forces or erosion (sea and stream) cut a second tunnel.

attention and concentration. I avoided the stream by traversing the rock wall on the left or north. The traverse took me only two to five inches above the water of Coast Creek. At higher tides one has to keep an eye on the breakers while heading away from the sea into the tunnel. If not, you get your feet wet which is no great tragedy but enough of a nuisance. Once my traverse was completed, I reached the cliff trail which runs some 60 yards up to Miller Point 30 vertical feet overhead.

On the Miller Point headland the usual cluster of Sunday hikers were eating a snack, snoozing in the late afternoon sun, or gazing out to sea. I joined them briefly, then took up the Coast Trail 50 yards to the east as it comes down from the hills. As I moved away from the sea I glanced up at the high hills immediately south of Bear Valley Creek. Sometimes one can catch a glimpse of deer grazing on the highest ridge. Before my eyes reached the highest hill my attention was caught by a fat bushy creature moving diagonally up the shaded portion of the hillside. Had the fox remained motionless I might not have seen it. I was struck with the bushiness of the tail and the uphill speed with which it soon disappeared in some brush beneath a large cave set in a rocky cliff.

On the Coast Trail, where it junctions with the Bear Valley Trail, I joined the groups of other hikers working their way homeward up Bear Valley. Soon we'd be covered by arching bay trees and protruding fir branches. Fringing the trail, blue forget-me-nots cheered the weary hikers. And the prickly nettle prodded those who slipped too far off the edge of the trail. In three and a half miles we'd gained almost 400' at the crest of Divide Meadow, the only truly open area along the Bear Valley Trail until the Bear Valley Trailhead. In the afternoon Divide Meadow is a kind of last rest stop for hikers and cyclists. Prostrate and slumbering bodies were scattered across the pine dotted upper meadow as I plopped down for a final snack. The meadow was in shade now and the warmth of the day was quickly dissipating.

Cutting my rest short, I donned a jacket and took up the last mile and a half to the Bear Valley Trailhead parking lot. The abrupt drop from the top of Divide Meadow gave me a "running start," and in less than half an hour I had passed through the densely wooded eastern half of Bear Valley to the Bear Valley Trailhead. Emerging from the forest and into the open some 300 yards from the parking lot, I looked out upon the prominent clump of hills I call "the knuckles" (Black Mountain) as it caught the waning rays of the afternoon sun. A string of weary hikers was making its way up the straight stretch of trail to the parking lot. There was still a touch of forest aroma in the cooling air. A very special spring day was coming to an end, and my sense of joy was enhanced by my knowledge that I would come back again and again.

Woodward Valley Trail, just above its junction with the Coast Trail.

Wildcat Beach and Alamere Falls from the Coast Trail.

CHAPTER 2

Bear Valley Trailhead (Olema) to Double Point

*Bear Valley Trailhead—Bear Valley Trail —
Glenn Trail—Coast Trail —Wildcat Camp
—Wildcat Beach —Alamere Falls —
Wildcat Beach —"Miller Cave" —Miller Point
—Bear Valley Trail —Bear Valley Trailhead.*

15 – 16 miles
Strenuous — Involves trail and off-trail
hiking as well as about 1000
vertical feet of hiking.

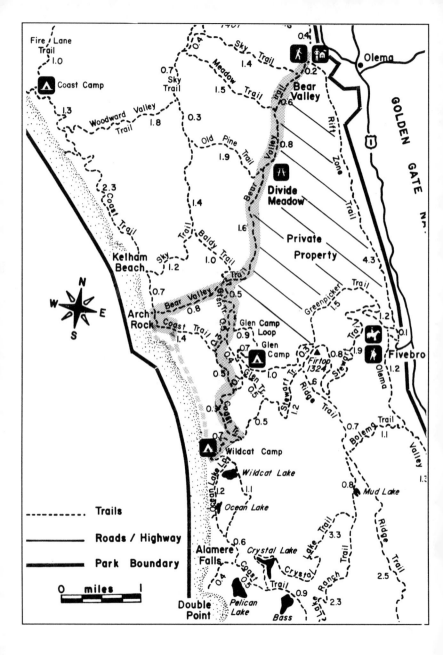

I t was March, and broken grey clouds suggested a possible rainstorm, as a friend and I set out down the Bear Valley Trail for Double Point. Expecting to cover many miles we got off to an early start from the Bear Valley Trailhead. With packs chuck full of food, camera gear, and rain clothing we moved down the Bear Valley Trail at better than 3.5 mph.

For the better part of the 1.6 miles to Divide Meadow we strode through the dense forest of bay, fir, oak, and madrone at an irregular pace. Recent rains had left numerous puddles on the road-trail so we were forced to hop, swerve, jump, and tip-toe over, around, and through the puddles to keep our feet dry. Just as we reached Divide Meadow the sun broke through momentarily to cheer us. There was no one at the meadow — human or animal — and we stopped for a moment to listen to the silence. Then on, and slightly downhill, towards the junction with the Glen Trail, another 1.6 miles away. Soon we were back in the forest avoiding puddles and nettle on the fringe of the trail.

At the junction of the Bear Valley Trail and the Glen Trail, 1.6 miles from Divide Meadow, we spotted a cluster of lady bugs on a dead log. Then we found another cluster nearby. Then another. An entire colony with orange shells with black specs. Most of the bugs remained motionless while a few nudged upwards, sideways, or backwards but a fraction of an inch. Why the creatures had picked a location so accessible to people puzzled me. The Bear Valley Trail is the most traveled trail in the Seashore. On a Sunday afternoon in spring and summer over 300 people come and go down this trail in a single day!

Leaving the lady bugs to their fate, we started up the steep road-trail known as the Glen Trail. In 300 yards and 300 vertical feet we came upon a slanting open meadow of soggy green grass. At the fringe of the meadow a grazing white stag[1] spotted us and meandered out of sight into the dark green forest.

In an other 500 yards of uphill hiking, now through the forest, we came upon the junction of the Glen Trail and the Glen Camp Loop Trail. We kept to the right and continued on the Glen Trail while the Glen Camp Loop Trail broke to the left towards Glen Camp one mile away. We continued upward through the Douglass fir forest. In about 300 yards we came upon a small open meadow where a now short unnamed trail (once called the Highland Loop Trail) came into the Glen Trail from the west at about a 90 degree angle. At this point we turned right (westward) onto the unnamed trail (a genuine trail in contrast to the Glen Trail, which is an old ranch road) and passed into a small but dense forest, only to emerge abruptly into open grasslands. Had we elected not to take the unnamed trail by remaining on the Glen Trail, we would have reached Glen Camp in about one mile of generally forested walking. Gradually our unnamed trail turned southwest and 300 to 400 yards brought us to the junction of the Coast Trail coming up from Miller Point and the sea some 700 feet and 1.4 hiking miles below.

We were in the favorite habitat of the white deer, some 750' above sea level. Here the deer feed on the lush grasslands of the open hills, and they bed down amid the clumps of coyote brush or under the fir forest east of the meadow. But the areas seemed deserted as we proceeded quietly through the green fields. Here and there clumps of wild flowers punctuated the open hillsides and sloping meadows.

---

[1]The Fallow stags have palmate antlers like moose.

The Coast Trail, which provides a magnificent view of Drakes Bay as it comes up from Miller Point, is now characterized by a broad meadow flanked by low hills covered with coyote brush to the east and a dense conifer forest to the southwest. We glided quickly through this section under gray skies and a light drizzle.

Looking over my shoulder to the northwest I saw the grey arm of Point Reyes itself jet out into the sea. It was shrouded in clouds and barely distinct. In 0.5 mile from where we picked up the Coast Trail, we came upon a "T" intersection. The Coast Trail turns right at this intersection. A left turn takes one back to the Glen Trail, which we had left 10 to 15 minutes earlier, through a conifer forest in 0.1 mile of easy walking. We turned right, or westward, still in open country, and proceeded about 400 yards to an imposing view of the sea. At this point the discontinued Old Coast Trail might be seen, somewhat overgrown, coming in from the right or northwest. Here we stood for a moment, gazing over the absolute calm of the sea far below as sunrays suddenly pierced the clouds and cast themselves on the surface of the water. We turned left or southward towards Wildcat Camp on the Coast Trail.

The descent to Wildcat Camp and Beach was spectacular. We dropped 800' in less than two miles. The view became panoramic. Some 600-700 yards from the point of our leaving the spot where the Coast Trail meets the Old Coast Trail we leveled off temporarily among some blackberry vines, coyote brush, and poison oak. To the right of this miniature and open plateau, some 100 yards away, was a group of conifers which hid, we soon discovered, some concrete gun emplacements. These had been erected by the United States Army during World War II to thwart a would-be Japanese invasion. The abandoned and dismantled forts, now covered, commanded a sweeping view of the sea some 500' below. Well hidden by the conifers, the forts were impregnable to direct assault from the beach. (The forts have since been closed up and covered with earth.)

Moving back onto the Coast Trail, we came upon an incredible view. 500' and almost directly below a road and flat meadow stretched westward to the sea with only the narrow beach between the meadow and the breakers. Wildcat Meadow (now Wildcat Camp), marked the terminus of a wooded ravine which plunged at right angles to our view. Cutting a deep canyon from the north, the ravine suddenly broadened and flattened out into the open meadow below us. Immediately south, rolling hills rose up and ran parallel to the coastline. These green hills undulated, almost totally free of conifers, until they culminated in the high hill at Double Point. The western face of this high hill fell abruptly into the sea over brownish-maroon sedementary rock. Wildcat Lake is nestled in the hills between Wildcat Meadow and the hill at Double Point, some 200 yards from the sea. Wildcat Meadow (Wildcat Camp) lay in a kind of sunken plateau between our high perch and the 480' hill at Double Point.

Descending abruptly towards Wildcat Meadow, we came suddenly upon another trail junction, another "T" intersection. Coming in from our left was the Stewart Trail, which originates at Five Brooks Trailhead some 4.7 miles from this point to the east. We turned right and continued downward to Wildcat Meadow and Wildcat Beach via the Coast Trail. In 1/2 mile from our junction we leveled out onto Wildcat Meadow.

Dense clumps of yellow mustard flower fringed the meadow, contrasting noticeably with the green meadow and uneven grey sky. We could hear the crash of breakers from just beyond the 10' rise marking the end of the meadow and the beginning of the beach 150 yards to the west. Two black buzzards sailed lazily over the wooded hills eastward reminding me that I was hungry, so we had lunch in the meadow.

The Coast Trail brushed the southern edge of Wildcat Meadow and crossed Wildcat Creek. We followed a small trail, branching off the Coast Trail, which parallels Wildcat Creek for about 150 yards down to the beach. We wanted to get inside the cove at Double Point[2] to see if we could find some marine mammals. We could have gone back to the Coast Trail and hiked southward towards Double Point Cove, but the beach route was most direct and a safer approach to the cove. Then, along the beach route, we could see Alamere Falls a mile and a quarter down Wildcat Beach. The recent rains promised to make it spectacular.

We were soon plodding in soft sand to avoid the high tide breakers which denied us a path of hard packed sand, the kind of sand one finds at low tide. Alamere Falls and the high cliff at Double Point beyond came immediately into view as we emerged from the log jam of drift wood where Wildcat Creek meets the beach. Squadrons of pelicans, keeping 50-70 feet off the water, flew over us from the south. And, scurrying lazily away from us as we drove them down the beach, groups of sanderlings and gulls refused to be stampeded into flight.

Alamere Falls, 40' high and 15 yards wide, was full and white. Alamere Creek splashed over the falls onto the sand through which it cut a swath six inches deep and some 10 feet wide straight to the

---

[2]The Park Service has since closed Double Point Cove from March 1 to June 30 because in this period seal pups are born and nurtured.

sea. From Alamere Falls one has the option of taking a side trip into Double Point Cove about 3/4 mile down the coast. The route is difficult in one section and requires climbing on steep exposed rock 30 feet above the sea. *This side trip should not be attempted except during a minus low tide and between July and January only.* Check the tide data at the Seashore Headquarters at Olema before hand. Also, one should be respectful of the fact that Double Point Cove is the home of a large herd of marine mammals. Now that travel within the cove is restricted (it wasn't in the early days of the National Seashore) by the Park Service one can use a fine vantage point above Double Point Cove. On a high hill (marked with "490" feet on the USGS 7 1/2 minute Double Point Topographical Map) just off the Coast Trail as it turns towards the sea at a point north of Pelican Lake one has a fine view of the marine mammals on the beach below. Only some 800 yards of cross country travel over open hills is involved.

That day my friend and I decided to look at the cove so we hurdled Alamere Creek and moved, in 200 yards, to the northern tip of Double Point. We scrambled up the rock. The route required a 30' to 40' diagonal climb on a somewhat broken face to a small "platform" from which we were able to see the rest of the route. From our platform, 30' above a receding medium tide, we did a diagonally descending traverse across good rock with solid and spacious foot and handholds to the edge of a short 6 foot cliff. At the bottom of the cliff there was a large flat boulder, solid but slippery wet from the high tide a few hours searlier. We navigated the six foot cliff by searching out holds, facing in, and letting ourselves down onto the flat rock at the base. The Double Point Cove, itself still remained hidden by a narrow belt of rock lying at the base of a high cliff leads some 600 yards around and into the cove. Scrambling over a few small boulders and onto the narrow rock belt leading on towards the cove, we looked to our right to see Stormy Stack, a barren island 300 yards off-shore. It was being spectacularly pounded by the surf.

Rounding into the cove, we beheld a narrow miniature bay with a thin curve of beach connecting the far points of Double Point. The southern point, directly across from us, couldn't have been more than 700 yards away. Falling onto the beach over a low cliff was Pelican Creek. The creek ran through a narrow ravine most of which was hidden. The waters of the cove were more placid than the ocean along Wildcat Beach behind us. But nowhere in the water or on the beach was there a trace of the marine mammals who are supposed to inhabit the cove. Low breakers seemed to come at shorter intervals and churned over large grains of black sand.

We stepped off the rocky belt onto the curving beach of the northern end of the cove. I noticed a pile of driftwood strewn across the beach about 300 yards away from us and beyond Pelican Falls. We studied the driftwood. So large. So concentrated. Suddenly one of the pieces of driftwood wiggled off the beach into the sea. Then the others followed in turn. In the next minute some 75 seals slithered into the cove. Once in the water they turned, popped their heads up, and studied us from 35-100 yards.

Pelican Creek comes cascading over a 50 foot cliff onto the beach at mid-cove. Erosion has altered the cliff so much that the route has become a dangerous obstacle. Consequently, I strongly recommend returning to Alamere Falls by the same route taken to get inside Double Point Cove.

There are two options for returning directly to the Bear Valley Trailhead. One is to return by the same route followed to Alamere

Falls from Bear Valley. This will be necessary during high tides since the northern half of Wildcat Beach will be difficult, perhaps impossible, to manage during plus high tides. At low tide one can begin the return to Bear Valley Trailhead by moving up Wildcat Beach towards Miller Point. That March day my companion and I, having returned to Wildcat Camp from Pelican Lake via the Coast Trail, found the tide medium, but fast receding so we chose a route up Wildcat Beach to Miller Point. If the tide was low we could slip through a large cave which, at medium and high tides, blocks the route to Miller Point from the northern end of Wildcat Beach. If the tide was too high, as is usually the case, we would take a cliff route from the beach to the Coast Trail (this cliff route parallels a small creek and is found about 200-300 yards from the southern promitory of Miller Point).

Moving northward up Wildcat Beach in the direction of Miller Point, we encountered magnificient cliffs of soil and rock. Here and there two and three foot piles of broken rock at the base of these cliffs reminded us of their instability. Occasionally springs came bounding down the cliffs from ledge to ledge. Perched on narrow ledges along the waterfalls bunches of yellow monkey flower were resplendent in the afternoon sunlight which had begun to break through the clouds. These seasonal waterfalls trickle down some 50-100 feet onto the beach. Abbreviated tunnels and sandy amphitheaters provided variety along the way, as did pelicans splashing into the sea onto unsuspecting fish from 100' above the water.

---

[3]This route is subject to considerable erosion during heavy winter and spring rains and may, in time, become more difficult than discussed here.

The tide was receding and we anticipated that the cave route at Miller Point would go. We therefore passed the cliff route,[3] marked by a clump of vegetation surrounding a spring which oozes down through a very shallow cliff. Going up the cliff route does not involve exposure to anything worse than a skinned knee or nettle sting. And in the lower going one gets sand in his or her shoes. The cliff route leads up some 150 yards and 300 vertical feet (at a 15-25 degree angle) to the old Coast Trail as it comes over the top of a small knoll overlooking Miller Point itself and to a fine view up the coastal shelf to the north. At the high point of the knoll a small headstone marks the grave of the late Clem Miller, the California State Senator whose efforts helped establish Point Reyes National Seashore. Thirty yards away you will see the current Coast Trail coming down from the hills to the northeast.

We scurried on another 150 yards along the sandy beach. The beach turned westward reaching out to form the southern tip of Miller Point. 70 yards of cautious boulder hopping on seaweed covered rocks, put us on a rocky cliff. This was easily traversed for about forty feet. A beautiful green tidepool waited to catch us if we fell. But the traverse was easy — plenty of good foot and handholds — and brought us quickly to a small hole in the cliff about 9 feet by 9 feet. An enormous log, which aided our completion of the traverse and passage through the hole in the rock wall, was jammed into the hole (the log is no longer there as of this date). Through the hole we passed to the mouth of the cave,[4] whose floor was covered with about one foot of lazily lapping water. The sides offered hand and footholds for an easy traverse into the far end of the cave which, though dripping from the recent innundation of high tide, was free

---

[4]The cave is impassable at high and medium tides.

of the ocean. We had no problem either in the traverse, which found us practically walking on the water, or in navigating the cave which I call "Miller Cave." Miller Cave is actually two small caves separated by a wall of rock. Both are so shallow they are fully lighted. Getting out of the cave requires one long step and one long reach for foot and hand holds in order to avoid a deep tidepool within the cave. Anyone who fell would simply get wet so it might be a good idea to relay cameras and day packs.

Bear Valley Trail at Divide Meadow.

Once out of Miller Cave and onto its northern lip, we traversed a low angle of rock to the small beach just below the Arch Rock

Overlook (Miller Point). From there a 75 yard walk put us on the shore of Coast Creek as it plunges through the Sea Tunnel.

We stayed on the southern shore of Coast Creek, climbed 10 feet up a rock cliff, which offered generous hand and footholds, to a point where we could easily boulder hop across the creek to a trail on the northern shore and up to the Miller Point headland (sometimes called Arch Rock Overlook, because of the good view to be found of Arch Rock, 100 yards off shore).

With 4.1 miles to go from Miller Point up Bear Valley to the Bear Valley trailhead, our starting point, we treated ourselves to 15 minutes rest in the late afternoon sun. Clouds cast broken shadows across the sea. A gentle wind whipped a few white caps. On the beach, 60 feet below, hikers were trudging down the sand towards Kelham Beach. I closed my eyes to listen to the muffled crash of breakers and to savour the pungent aroma of fresh spring grass.

Meadow at the Bear Valley Trailhead.

CHAPTER 3

The Meadow—
Old Pine Trails Loop

Bear Valley Trailhead — Bear Valley Trail — Meadow Trail — Sky Trail — Old Pine Trail — Bear Valley Trail — Bear Valley Trailhead.

6 to 7 miles
Easy — Involves 1000 feet of gradual climbing through mostly forested regions.

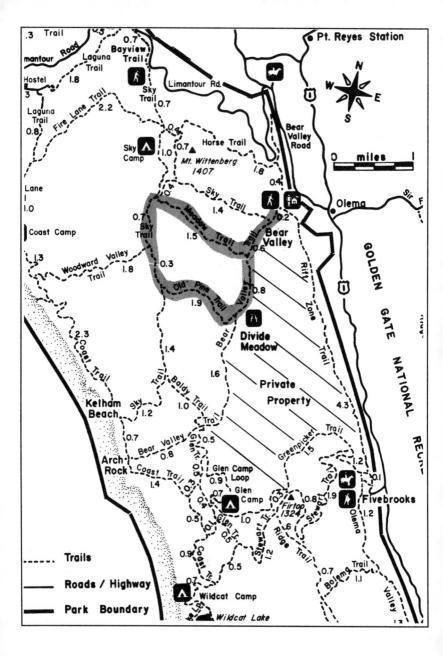

O rdinarily I prefer a hike which includes as much geographical-topographical variety as possible. And Point Reyes National Seashore is certainly the place for that. But for those who love the forest, or for those who want a short hike, or for those who love solitude and silence, this is the hike.

Begin at the Bear Valley Trailhead on, say a hot August morning. Go up Bear Valley (see Chapter 2) through the shade of the trees to the Meadow Trail junction 0.8 mile from the Bear Valley Trailhead. The Meadow Trail is another road-trail, an old ranch road, and it starts up quite steeply. Arching bay trees, madrone trees with peely bark, and stately Douglas firs with grey-green beards of Spanish moss shade the route.

After less than 1/2 mile and about 400 vertical feet of hiking, I broke out onto a sunlit meadow 200 yards wide. It slanted upward at about 15-20 degrees, the average incline of the Meadow Trail. The grass is usually green here even in August, but the sun was hot this day. I longed to reach the shade at the far end of the meadow. A fir forest fringes the meadow offering shady rest spots for lunch or for quiet contemplation. One can walk off into the woods here, sit down and have the entire forest all to oneself.

Beyond the upper end of the meadow I walked back into the shade of the forest. The trail continued upward, narrow and fringed with huckleberry bushes, now ripe, and ferns. Occasionally toyons, alders, and California holly crushed in along the edges of the trail. 1 1/2 miles from the bottom at Bear Valley and 1000 vertical feet up, the Meadow Trail comes abruptly on the junction with the Sky Trail. Right at the junction I found a familiar miniature meadow, fresh, green, and cool. Resisting the temptation to stop and rest on the soft green grass, I wheeled left and south along the Sky Trail towards its junction with the Woodward Valley Trail (see Chapter 1). Beyond the Woodward Valley Trail junction the Sky Trail rises sharply for about 100 yards and some 150-200 vertical feet before leveling and then climbing more gradually again. Then, 0.7 mile later, I suddenly came upon the Old Pine Trail junction. The Sky Trail, on which I was hiking, veered slightly right and level. I followed the Old Pine Trail up and slightly left into an even deeper forest.

I have seldom seen anyone on the Old Pine Trail[1] — weekdays or on weekends. Though the forest undergrowth is dense, one has no trouble in slipping 50-100 yards off the trail to find a resting spot. The silence is utter and the feeling is of absolute intimacy with nature. One is surrounded by a world of delicate green branches and stems. Now and then a bird flits silently from one branch to another or darts straight through the forest. On the forest floor insects climb over and under leaves, twigs, and plants in a world so alien to the world of people. If one waits long enough a group of deer may step softly through the forest enroute to some green meadow beyond. Lonely shadows cast by the trees break up patches of sunlight on the forest floor. The fir aroma is sweet in the warm air of summer and in the serenity and solitude one is lost in reveries of yesterday, today, and tomorrow.

The Old Pine Trail turns southeast, dropping at about 20-25 degrees in a few places. The total length of the trail, from its junction with the Sky Trail until it meets the Bear Valley Trail, is 1.9 miles. In the last 200 yards of the wooded trail one can hear, but not see, hikers and picnickers at Divide Meadow along the Bear Valley Trail. Then

---

[1]The Old Pine Trail is named for a small grove of Bishop Pines in a predominately Douglas fir forest!

On the Meadow Trail.

30 yards from Divide Meadow, the Old Pine Trail breaks abruptly out of the forest and into the open. 1.6 miles eastward on the Bear Valley Trail takes the hiker to the Bear Valley Trailhead.

On the Bear Valley Trail, I dodged a pack of cyclists coming up to the meadow from the Bear Valley Trailhead and began picking up the pace for the final 1.6 miles to the parking lot.

The Meadow Trail-Old Pine Trail Loop isn't so much a hike as it is a serene and intimate experience with pure wilderness. One can hike or run through it, but to experience it takes time and a willingness to sit quietly and alone in some quiet corner of this primeval wood.

Sky Trail on the way to Mount Wittenberg.

CHAPTER 4

The Limantour Loop

*Bear Valley Trailhead — Sky Trail —
Fire Lane — Coast Trail — Limantour Beach
— Coast Trail — Bear Valley Trail —
Bear Valley Trailhead.*

21 – 23 miles
Strenuous

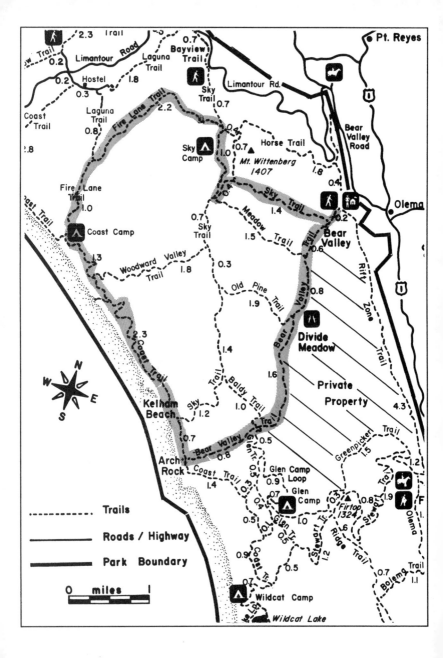

One April, a friend, who is a rugged hiker and climber, and I set out on a clear cool spring day from the Bear Valley Trailhead for a good hike. Our destination was the mouth of Drakes Estero on the Limantour spit. This we intended to accomplish by lunch, planning to turn around and return to Bear Valley Trailhead via a different route so as to be back in time for dinner at one of the numerous fine restaurants in Olema or Point Reyes Station. We turned off the Bear Valley Trail onto the Sky Trail to green meadows, wildflowers, stately Douglas firs, the serenade of birds, and the sweet scent of the woods.

As we reached the top of Mount Wittenberg we were overcome by the glory of the day. Wildflowers were just beginning to come up everywhere — tidy tips, lupines, paint brush. The air was clean and sweet, and Drakes Bay sparkled and danced in the sharp breeze which cut across its surface. Going cross country we dropped some 150' to the Mount Wittenberg Trail running generally north-south just below the summit of Mount Wittenberg. Crossing the Mount Wittenberg Trail, we dropped about 250 vertical feet to a second trail, the Sky Trail, which led us straight into Sky Camp some 100 yards from where we came down the hill to intersect the Sky Trail.

The meadow at Sky Camp was open, level, and commanded a fine view of Drakes Bay. We stopped for a moment to enjoy the surroundings and then took up the trail as it headed northward to a junction with the Fire Lane Trail 3/4 mile ahead. The Fire Lane takes 3.2 miles to reach Coast Camp over open terrain. After pausing for a few pictures, we moved on.

On this particular morning we saw a number of blacktail deer grazing in the meadows as we approached along the trail. The air was clean and cool which enabled us to see, in sharp relief, the brownish-white cliffs of Drakes Bay. The cliffs were some eight miles away but in the clear atmosphere they seemed closer. Whitecaps on the bay told us the westerlies had come up already. Here and there a cobweb stretched between two plant stems, sparkled with dew amid the grass still wet in the morning dampness. Clumps of iris and occasional crimson Indian paint brush broke the endless pattern of green on open ridges and meadows.

The Fire Lane took us through open country heavily vegetated with coyote brush, occasional blackberry vines and poison oak. What appeared to be a red-tailed hawk circled above Coast Camp at about our altitude (300 feet), and 1/4 mile to the west. Two white fawns (fallow deer) were already bounding away from us down the hillside when we first saw them. The deer pick up sounds and scents more readily than they see.

After 2.2 miles, the Fire Lane junctions with the Laguna Trail coming in from the north (right) and can be followed to the Point Reyes Hostel 1.1 miles away. Moving on, we found the Fire Lane developing a more gentle angle of descent in the last 3/4 mile before Coast Camp. At a large open meadow the trail leveled off and we found ourselves on the shore of a small seasonal pond on which a few ducks were swimming about.

With the sound of big combers crashing on the beach just ahead, we came to the Coast Trail junction at a point immediately northwest of Coast Camp by about 80 yards (Coast Camp itself is situated on a small meadow behind the low cliffs overlooking the sandy beach 100 to 150 yards west of the campsites via a small access trail). A sharp wind greeted us and we donned sweaters and windbreakers. Wind is the rule in springtime along the beaches of

Drakes Bay. It comes up around 9 to 10 a.m., blows mildly, then gains strength in the afternoon. Usually the wind drops off and stops by nightfall only to resume the cycle the next day.

We turned northwest along the beach towards Drakes Estero five miles into the wind. Suddenly we looked up to see a flock of geese flying north 200' overhead. And then a second squadron followed. And a third. As we moved along the wind-swept beach, grey-colored willets took to flight from along the edge of the surf. They headed straight towards the breakers, then banked downwind, and accelerated on the steady blast of cold air. The single white stripe on the willet's wings distinguishes it from seagulls, which are just as numerous along Drakes beach.

We soon pulled even with the scattered beach houses of the now defunct Drakes Bay Estates, a housing development project arrested some years ago by the establishment of Point Reyes National Seashore. Beyond the beach homes, now occupied by park personnel, we approached the opening of Drakes Estero. We turned into the dunes for shelter from the wind and to take our lunch. We were on Limantour Spit which jets westward for 3 1/2 miles from its anchor about a mile northwest of Santa Maria Beach and Coast Camp.

Following lunch we explored the mud flats along the north shore of Limantour Spit and worked our way westward about 500 yards to the mouth of Drakes Estero. In 1579 Sir Francis Drake, according to generally accepted but not undisputed theory, sailed his Golden Hinde vessel through the mouth of the Estero for a careenage somewhere on the sheltered shore opposite us. Gazing across the open landscapes west and north, I imagined that the scene could well have looked identical in 1579. From my vantage point at the tip of Limantour Spit I could see few hints of humankind — a ranch house and a few cows were the only things suggesting human intrusion.

Turning eastward, we cut across the low dunes dividing the mud flats of Limantour Spit from the ocean beach along Drakes Bay and headed on downwind towards the mouth of Bear Valley 7 miles from the western tip of Limantour Spit. Small grains of wind bourne sand raced past us just a few inches off the beach. White caps danced wildly on the brilliant surface of the sea. The afternoon sun had moved westward so that it began to illuminate the breakers from behind. The big boomers were nearly transparent as they surged up and crested over. Each surging wall of water was greenish in color and we could see masses of brownish sand suspended in the rising breakers just before they crested and crashed. The wind whipped a fine spray of mist off the breaker crests just before they turned downward. Our progress down the beach back to Coast Camp was slowed as we became absorbed in the ocean drama before us.

At Coast Camp we left the windy beach and the stinging sand to take up the Coast Trail. Our plan was to stay on the Coast Trail all the way — four miles — to the mouth of Bear Valley rather than to alternate by moving along the beach from time to time.

For most of its length (from the Hostel, formerly Laguna Ranch, to the mouth of Bear Valley) the Coast Trail parallels Drakes Bay. The trail moves across a natural shelf between the tops of the sea cliffs on the west and the base of the sharply rising hills to the east. The trail contours to avoid deep ravines cut by four southwest running creeks between Coast Camp and the mouth of Bear Valley. We escaped the stinging sand of this unusually gusty March day, but on the exposed shelf we found no respite from the wind. Where the Coast Trail crossed the four creeks mentioned we did find shelter by slipping into the forests of bay trees which generally terminate at the point of contact with the Coast Trail.

Heading southeastward on the Coast Trail, we caught glimpses of white deer grazing on the grassy slopes to our left and northeastward. And from time to time Double Point and Alamere Falls, four to five miles down the beach, came into view. As the Coast Trail passed by Point Resistance we left it temporarily to walk out onto the headland for a better view of the unnamed rock (I call it "Resistance Rock") to view the variety of bird life. The rock is the home of many seabirds, including pelicans ranging Drakes Beach. The chatter of birds which one can hear from the Coast Trail on a less windy day, could easily be heard above the wind at this point.

Then back onto the Coast Trail from the tip of point Resistance headland (200 yards) and on to Bear Valley Trail. Half a mile up Bear Valley we escaped all traces of the wind and took our first sitting break since leaving Limantour Spit some eight miles back. The hush of the forest was a welcome change from the constant rumbling of the wind. Only the faint mirthful gurgle of Coast Creek, running through Bear Valley, intruded upon the silence. With some 18 miles behind us, we especially enjoyed the respite.

McClures Beach as seen from near the trail between
the McClures Beach Trailhead and Tomales Point.

CHAPTER 5

The Tomales Point Loop

*Tomales Point Trailhead — Pierce Ranch Trail
— Tomales Point — west shore Tomales Bay
— Upper Pierce Ranch —
Tomales Point Trailhead.*

**9 – 10 miles
Moderate**

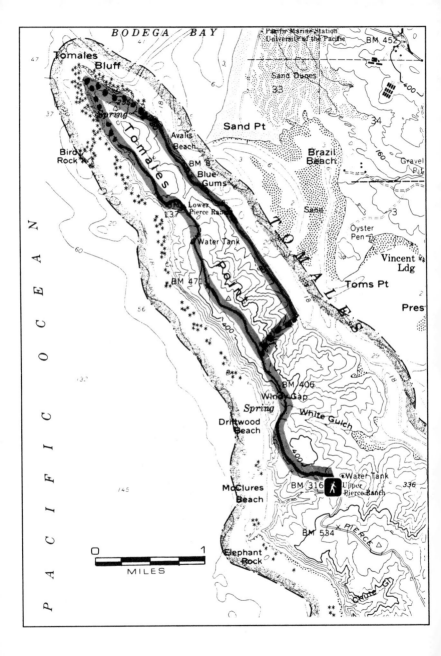

A t the northern tip of Point Reyes National Seashore a prominent peninsula protrudes northwestward between the Pacific Ocean and the long arm of Tomales Bay (Tomales Bay inundates a depressed section of the San Andreas earthquake fault-line and would make an island of the seashore area, as it once did, if it extended about 12 more miles to Bolinas Lagoon). A fascinating hike is to circumvent the narrow peninsula, a 10 to 11 mile trek involving trail and off-trail hiking.

On a balmy spring day a few years ago I took a group to McClures Beach, about 15 road miles from the Bear Valley Trailhead. We parked the cars at the parking area and picked up the road-trail which heads northward towards the tip of the peninsula at Tomales Bluff 4.5 miles away. We traveled on generally level and entirely open terrain, the highest point being 471' above sea level.

Occasionally we left the trail to walk 100 yards or so to the edge of the ocean cliffs facing the Pacific Ocean in hopes of searching out a beach route below. Not only were there few if any safe hiking routes down to the beach, but the beach below was dissected by proturding cliffs which appeared to block passage along the beach even at the lowest of tides. Subsequent attempts on my part to pass from McClures Beach to Tomales Bluff by a beach route have been thwarted by these uncompromising rock cliffs and almost non-existant beaches. From our cliff's edge viewpoint we observed numerous offshore rocks, many of which harbored birds and seals. The surf, which pounded these offshore rocks, was visible by the swirl of white water splashing around and, in some cases, over them.

Here and there along our road-trail, clumps of rotted granitic rock broke through the sandy soil. On such an outcrop, not far from

Tomales Bluff, we had our lunch. To the northeast the far shore of Tomales Bay was often visible as we continued towards Tomales Bluff along the road-trail which ran out about 1.5 miles from Tomales Bluff. Continuing off-trail involved hiking through open, level, and sandy terrain while dodging numerous clumps of yellow lupine (blooms in May and June).

Tomales Bluff itself stood less than 100' above the surf. Below the bluff a cluster of desolate weather worn rocks marked the shoreline and seemed to defy the oncoming breakers which came row upon row against them. Directly north and northwest the waters of Bodega Bay were whitecapped in the rising breeze. Far to the north tiny white dots of fishing boats marked Bodega Cove and harbor. Small offshore reefs cut across the southern end of Bodega Bay like so many giant stepping stones.

We turned southeast on open hills and hiked to a narrow beach (Avalis Beach) which was readily accessible and some 1000 to 1200 yards from Tomales Point. From this point the shoreline along the west edge of Tomales Bay[1] consists of a narrow beach interrupted from time to time by short rock protrusions which divide what would otherwise be a continuous beach into sections. We passed these rock protrusions, which extend from small 3 foot to 10 foot cliffs, by wading ankle-deep to knee-deep around them in calm water.[2] There was no problem with the six inch "breakers" along this sheltered shore, though some in our party preferred to wade in their tennis shoes because of occasional sharp rocks.

---

[1] It is strongly recommended that the return beach route to the Tomales Point Trailhead not be attempted in anything higher than a +2.0 tide. Check at the Seashore Headquarters beforehand to obtain tide information for Tomales Bay.

[2] Tomales Bay occasionally has sharks. Please be advised that you wade at your own risk.

The terrain above and beyond the cliffs consisted of gently upward rolling hills covered with brush and sparce clumps of scrub trees. The vegetation on this side of Tomales Bluff, was much more dense than on the west side and not inviting to cross country travel. Absent from view were the conifers so characteristic of the National Seashore between the Point Reyes Hostel and the southern boundary just north of Bolinas. In fact, there are few conifers anywhere in the area from McClures Beach to Tomales Bluff.

A variety of waterbirds were visisble off-shore as we alternately walked the beach and waded in the shallow water around the rock protrusions breaking the continuity of the beach. Many small creeks originating from low gradient gullies inland, poured out onto the sands and into the bay.

At a point 2 3/4 miles from Tomales Point, along the west shore of Tomales Bay where there is a small beach where moss covered cypress and a few eucalyptus are seen directly behind the narrow beach, turn inland and head for the Pierce Ranch Trailhead/ Tomales Point Trail which you followed to Tomales Point earlier in the day. This will be reached after a few hundred yards of bush whacking through coyote brush and occasional patches of poison oak. It is advisable to wear long pants for this stretch.

I suggest that you do not continue southeastward down the coast from the point of inland departure (the beach with the mossy cypress and eucalyptus, which is about 2 3/4 miles from Tomales Point). Even at low tide you would be forced, at one point, to wade chest high in murky water along sheer cliffs of 15 to 30 feet.

The round trip hike from the Pierce Ranch Trailhead to Tomales Point and back via the Tomales Bay coast, as described, is 10 to 11 miles. What it lacks in topographical variety it makes up for in wildlife. Sometimes whales can be seen from the Pacific Ocean side of the hills. More common are deer, foxes, numerous rodents, rabbits and, along Tomales Bay, seals and a variety of sea birds including blue herons, cormorants, gulls, pipers and others. In the early 1980's a mountain lion was sighted in the Tomales headlands north of the parking area. A pair of binoculars is recommended to give you a better look at the wildlife in this very open country.

On Tomales Point Trail by moonlight.

Open meadow along the Sky Trail

CHAPTER 6

Bear Valley Trailhead
Sky Trail
Bear Valley Loop

Bear Valley Trailhead — Sky Trail —
Coast Trail — Bear Valley Trail —
Bear Valley Trailhead.

10 – 11 miles — 1400 feet of trail climbing.
Moderate

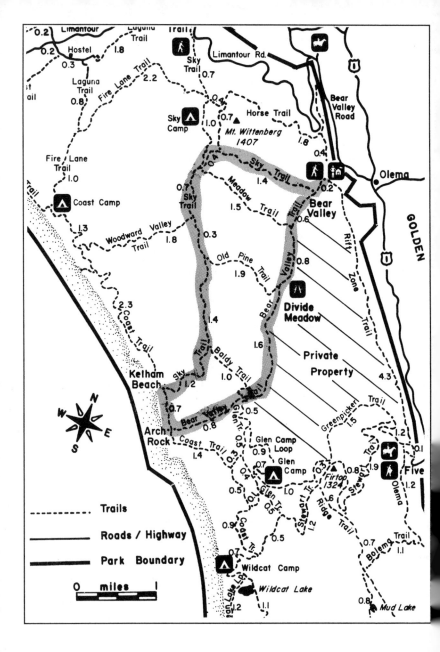

T hose who want the shortest possible hike with the maximum variety of terrain try this one. You'll have immediate uphill, plenty of downhill, yet mostly level hiking. In this eleven mile hike you'll have just about everything Point Reyes National Seashore has to offer.

You start from the Bear Valley Trailhead and take the Sky Trail off the Bear Valley Trail. Proceed on the Sky Trail along the Inverness Ridge to the junction with first the Meadow Trail (1.9 miles from Bear Valley Trailhead and 1000 feet elevation) and then the Old Pine Trail (2.5 miles from Olema Trailhead).

Beyond the Old Pine Trail junction, the Sky Trail continues its nearly due southward direction through dense conifers, huckleberries, thimbleberries, madrones, bays, ferns, and toyons on the Inverness Ridge. The first time I ever hiked the Sky Trail in its entirety, I was struck by the sudden emergence onto open sunlit hills of green grass sprinkled liberally with wild oats. And almost as soon as I broke out of the forest, 1 1/2 miles south of the Old Pine Trail junction, the Sky Trail dipped and rose sharply to an open grassy knoll. Leaving the trail and stepping 30 yards to the west, I crested the knoll to discover a magnificent view of Drakes Bay and much of the region south of Kelham Beach. A perfect lunch stop — well off the trail, with an outstanding panoramic view.

From my vista point I returned to the Sky Trail which began an increasingly steep drop. In one mile's hiking I was to drop 750' to the Coast Trail below, and most of that drop took place in the last 1/4 mile. While descending through open and rolling meadows I enjoyed an intimate view of the regions from Point Resistance to Double Point. As the trail turned westward to move into a small grove of bays and oaks, I looked to my left and south to observe a band of white deer grazing on a grassy knoll studded with tall thistles and coyote brush. Using the coyote brush as a screen, I crawled from bush to bush in futile attempts to get close enough for a good telephoto picture. I was upwind from the band and the last I saw of them they were 100 yards away and running.

Picking up the Sky Trail[1] again, I slipped through the small grove of bay and oak, emerged into the open again some 100 feet downtrail, and came upon my first view of the Coast Trail 400 feet below stretching at right angles to my line of descent. In a few minutes I bounded down onto the Coast Trail, turned right, and some 300 yards later reached the small footpath which leads to Kelham Beach 150 yards off the Coast Trail. Here on the warm and nearly deserted sands I stretched out, closed my eyes, and listened to the concert of the surf until I fell asleep.

After my nap I awoke to notice that the low tide had become even lower during my sleep. This gave me an opportunity to explore the large cave 300 yards up (northwest) the beach. The cave, navigatable only at low tide, was dripping from its 20 foot ceiling as I worked my way towards a small opening some 50 feet at the far end of the cave. As I progressed toward the small opening the cave ceiling became lower, and I had to crouch low to pass through the opening and onto a secluded semi-circle of beach. The beach, narrow and wet, was surrounded on three sides by the sheer walls of Point Resistence which cradles it. The beach itself was no more than 30 to 35 yards across.

---

[1]For an alternate route back to Bear Valley, take the Old Baldy Trail off Sky Trail. The Old Baldy Trail descends through the forest to Bear Valley at the junction of the Bear Valley Trail and the Glen Trail. This alternate route shortens the hike by about one mile.

From Kelham Beach back to Bear Valley Trailhead the two most direct return options open to me were: 1) proceeding down the beach (southeast) 3/4 mile to the Sea Tunnel, through the small, usually navigable tunnel, and up onto the Bear Valley Trail via the footpath just past the "inside" end of the Sea Tunnel. The foot path takes one to Miller Point directly over the tunnel and then, over open grassslands, to the Coast Trail 300 yards from Miller Point. 2) proceeding to the Coast Trail via the footpath from Kelham Beach and moving southeastward in open country about one mile to where the Coast Trail breaks to the right as a footpath and the Bear Valley Trail breaks left as the same road trail. From this junction it would be 4 miles of woods and meadows back to the Bear Valley Trailhead.

On Sculptured Beach.

Off the Sunset Beach Trail.

CHAPTER 7

The Estero Region

*Estero Region parking lot — Home Bay —
Estero de Limantour — Home Bay —
Estero Region parking lot*

**8 – 9 miles
Easy**

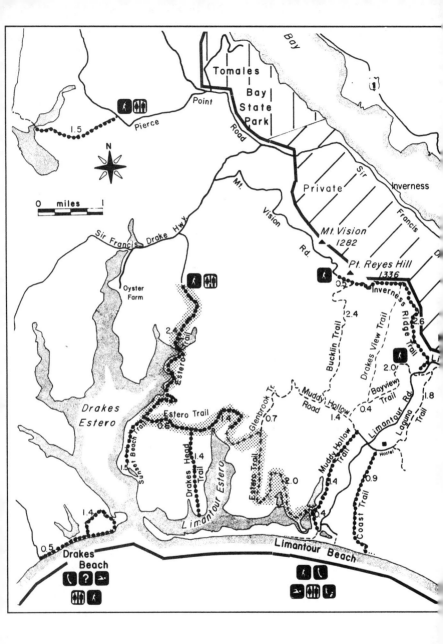

T he Estero region, situated in the northwest corner of Point Reyes National Seashore, has no broad beaches, no ocean caves, no waterfalls or natural lakes, no deep forests or high hills. Yet it is distinctive. For it has sweeping moors reminiscent of Scotland. And wildlife, abundant and highly visible—bobcats, Axis deer, Fallow deer, Blacktail deer, marsh hawks, white pelicans, a variety of geese, cormorants, herons, and egrets. Out on the low tide sand bars colonies of seals sun themselves for an hour or two. In spring lupine, paint brush, asters, tidy tips, and monkey flower are abundant but clumps of Douglas iris are dominant starting as early as February.

There is a network of trails throughout the Estero region. They provide, thus, a variety of hikes having various distances. The main artery of this trail network is the Estero Trail.

THE ESTERO TRAIL

The Point Reyes administration had recently revised the Estero Trail[1] so, needing to update this chapter and being curious about what new areas it might lead me to, I set out to do the Estero Trail twice before turning to my pen. Once in the spring and again in autumn.

I began at the broad hillside immediately west of the Estero Trail (parking lot is .7 mile from Francis Drake Blvd.) On my spring hike clumps of iris had greeted me frequently all along the 8-9 mile hike, whereas in fall the purple flowers were gone and the plants had

[1]The new Estero Trail is simply a rerouted trail using, in most cases, an old ranch road long ago put in by ranchers.

turned partly a brown-rust color. The perennial coyote brush remained—dominant in scattered thickets and blossoming in fall. Easily seen in both seasons were the white Fallow deer, grazing either solitary or in small groups of 6 or 7. In fall I came closer to Axis deer, which confine themselves to this area of the National Seashore, more than ever before. Axis deer are characterized by white spots on tan bodies, white lower legs, and, with the stags, horns shaped more like gazelles than those of the California Blacktail deer. On my autumn hike of the Estero Trail I surprised a bobcat which had been lurking nearby. In both seasons Blue Herons and egrets stalked the mud flats along Drakes Estero at lowtide. And in the Limantour Estero a squadron of 6 or 7 white pelicans majestically sailed high and away during my fall excursion. Cormorants, wings flapping with characteristic fury, dashed across Drakes Estero low to the water to avoid the stiff springtime winds. A marsh hawk buzzed me on the downwind during my April hike, but the two I saw in autumn were barely discernable as they soared over the shore of Limantour Estero. Blacktail deer were frequently seen in the coyote brush in both seasons. Seagulls, of course, were constantly riding the airways of the western edges of Drakes and Limantour Esteros.

The Estero Trail—in its present condition—is no easy trail to follow. For nearly half its length it is obscure. In some places there is no discernable trail to follow—only directional arrows on posts a few of which have fallen. Therefore, some detailed description is necessary here.

The Estero Trail is 9 miles one way. The hiker is faced with an 18 mile round trip if he or she wishes to return to the Estero Trailhead. So it it best to drop off a pick-up vehicle at Limantour Beach parking lot so that the hike can be done one way. This will give ample time to watch for wildlife. Or the hiker can combine the first few miles of the Estero Trail with some of the region's other trails (discussed later in this chapter).

After leaving the parking lot at the trailhead, the Estero Trail becomes an up and down old ranch road which bridges the east end of Drakes Estero (you can watch the tide rushing in or out from the bridge). Then it climbs and dips until, 2.4 miles from the trailhead, it makes a 90 degree left or eastward turn. A trail sign informed me that if I continued straight ahead (south) I would be traveling on the Sunset Beach Trail[2] which would put me on the Limantour Estero shore in 1.5 miles of easy walking. Had I proceeded to Sunset Beach I would have had Drakes Estero almost constantly in view to my right (west). And a small, usually deserted, sandy beach nestled between cliffs rising sheer out of the waters of Limantour Estero. However, I chose the Estero Trail and turned left onto what is the semi cross country section of the route. Moving, thus, in an eastward direction and up a gently rising grass slope I found no discernable trail. Then, in about 100 yards from the junction just behind me, I came upon a simple post with a white directional arrow on a blue background directing me to continue east. Then, in another 200-250 yards my cross country route took me to a barbed wire fence with which the now faintly discernable trail merged so that the two were parallel with the fence on the right. In still another 200 plus yards a trail sign directed me through a turnstile gate. Once through the fence, I encountered a second fence leading in the direction of a wooden tower standing almost 20 feet high. The trail, now a faint cowpath, paralleled this

---

2 The Sunset Beach Trail was once part of the original Estero Trail.

second fence on which a directional sign had been placed roughly 200 yards from the turnstile behind me. At a point close to the wooden tower I encountered yet another turnstile opening and passed on through the second fence. All the while a large rusted water tank, resting on its side some 200 yards to the right, or southward, was visible.[3] I now found myself on a broad hill crown and still traveling eastward parallel to yet another fence, the third one, towards still another fence some 500 yards dead ahead and running at right angles to my direction. At this fourth fence I encountered both an open gate and a turnstile. Passing through this fence I noticed a trail and the Drakes Head trail. Had I chosen the Drakes Head Trail, as I have many times before, I would have traveled south over open country towards a clump of conifers about a mile from the trail junction. Just .4 mile beyond the conifers the Drakes Head Trail, an old cow path, comes to the edge of a bluff over looking Limantour Estero, the cliffs of Drakes Beach, and much of Drakes Bay itself.

From the bluff I have, on past occassions, retraced my steps for some 200-250 yards to descend, northward, to a very private beach situated immediately west of the Drakes Head bluff. A round trip hike from the Estero Trailhead to Drakes Head and back is a modest 9.6 mile trip across generally level moors—an especially fine trip amid spring flowers.

---

[3]This tank has been in this position since the early 70's though it is possible that some day the dairy rancher who leases this area of the Estero region from the U. S. Government will move it.

From the Estero-Drakes Head trails junction[4] I continued east having picked up yet another fence (a shallow cement water trough is situated close to the junction). In about 60 yards from the junction a barely discernable trail sign (directional arrow) sent me through the fence as a series of parallel cow paths ran northwest, away from the fence, and downhill towards the eastern end of Limantour Estero 400 plus yards away. At last trail markers— directional arrows in white mounted on posts—became more numerous and the route clearer. [5] I thus proceeded along the west shore of Limantour Estero to a land bridge running east-west and separating the Estero from a fresh water lake on the other side (north) of the land bridge (this small lake is not shown on the Park Service hand-out map). Passing Limantour Estero, I saw Blue Herons and white pelicans during my autumn hike of the Estero Trail. In spring an egret stalked the low tide mud flats of the Estero while numerous ducks congregated on the lake.

At the eastern end of the land bridge I encountered yet another fence complete with turnstile and directional arrow sign. So I followed on the east shore of the Limantour Estero in a southerly direction. The trail became surrounded by thick blackberry, thimbleberry, and poison oak. All have been sufficiently cut back

---

[4] The trail sign reads: "Glenbrook Trail   1.4

Muddy Hollow Trail 3.4

Drakes Head   1.4"

I believe that the estimates for Glenbrook Trail junction and the Muddy Hollow Trail junction are inaccurate. I estimate that the Glenbrook junction is 1.8 or 2 miles away and that Muddy Hollow junction is more like 3.8 or 4 miles away.

[5] Be alert. The sign posts sometimes collapse during heavy winter rains.

though I realized that this section of the Estero Trail (some 350 yards in length) could easily overgrow unless periodically trimmed.

Eventually (400 yards) the trail evolved from footpath into an ancient but discernable ranch road which began a gentle climb from the Limantour Estero in a northerly direction. In about 3/4 mile I came upon the Glennbrook Trail junction. The Glennbrook Trail appeared to be another old ranch road. It is perhaps the shortest trail in the National Seashore—0.7 miles in length. It connects the Estero Trail to Muddy Hollow Road which, itself an old ranch road, leads to Muddy Hollow and the Point Reyes Hostel (2.2 miles to the Hostel from Glennbrook-Estero Trails junction).

I now turned south as the Estero Trail continued to snake its way over entirely open country. Moving along I could see the sands of Limantour Beach across Limantour Estero. To the west the cliffs of Drakes Bay rose sheer and bright in the brilliant light of spring but dull and somber on the foggy day of my mid October hike. In 800 yards I found the trail gradually turning me 180 degrees. Thus I was soon heading due north instead of due south (the Estero Trail is the most circuitous trail in Point Reyes National Seashore). No sooner had I made the sweeping change in direction on my autumn hike but a bobcat, startled by my sudden approach, bounded across the grass. It had apparently been eating the carcass of a recently dead Blacktail stag. Beyond the dead deer I came upon a grove of eucalyptus looking very much out of place here on the coyote brush covered moors.

The trail now turned east through a marsh and alder thicket. Then, catching me off guard, the path turned 90 degrees left, or north, immediately past the bridge which crosses the wettest part of the marsh. At this point I actually missed the rather obscure turn and spent a few minutes floundering in search of the trail in the tall grass straight ahead from the bridge. Discovering the trail, I followed it into the alder thicket for about 100 yards before breaking out, again, in open country. The Estero Trail then began a winding climb up a 300 foot hill to a broad and flat summit. Fully in view, now, were Muddy Hollow and the fresh water pond at its western terminus. The pond is separated from the Limantour marsh lands by a land bridge. Numerous ducks, startled by my sudden emergence from the alders surrounding the land bridge fluttered and flapped away in a rising formation. A Blue Heron, however, chose to ignore me from but 70 yards away. Then, in .4 mile, I came abruptly upon Limantour Beach parking lot to complete a 9 mile hike across the bush covered moors of the unique Estero region.

For those accustomed to the forested and rugged coastal areas typical of central and southern Point Reyes National Seashore the Estero Region offers a considerably different environment which is lightly traveled and possessing highly visible wildlife.

Mud Lake on the Lake Ranch Trail.

CHAPTER 8

The Five Brooks –
Lake Ranch Loop

*Five Brooks Trailhead — Stewart Trail —
Greenpicker Trail — Stewart Trail —
Coast Trail — Lake Ranch Trail —
Bolema Trail — Olema Valley Trail*

---

14 – 15 miles
Moderate – Strenuous
— Involves climbing about 1000 feet twice.

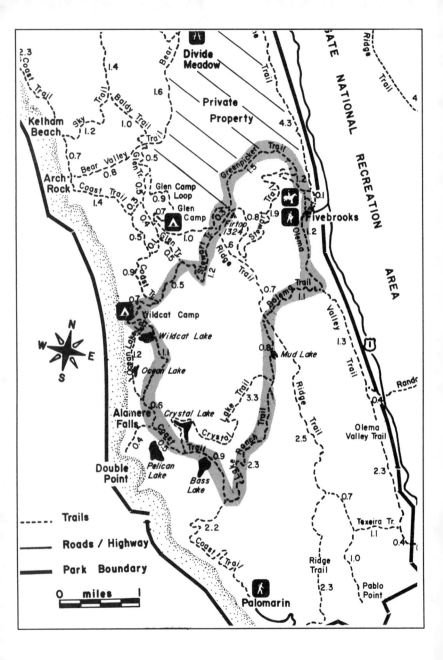

O n a bright Sunday morning in early spring I took off up the Stewart Trail out of the Five Brooks Trailhead at a good clip. Moving through the deep forest of Douglas fir for a mile and a half, I came upon the junction of the Stewart Trail and the Greenpicker Trail. Both trails lead up to the Ridge Trail slightly over 1000 vertical feet above Five Brooks. The climb to the Ridge Trail is about 2.8 miles by either trail from Five Brooks. Figure three miles via the Stewart Trail and 2.8 miles by branching off the Stewart Trail and taking the Greenpicker Trail. Both trails climb up somewhat steeply through the deep forest. On this particular morning I chose to take the Greenpicker Trail. The Greenpicker Trail is narrower than the Stewart Trail. It appears to have been a ranch road many years ago for it is much overgrown, whereas the Stewart Trail is still used by the Park Service for vehicular patrol out to Wildcat Camp.

On the Greenpicker Trail I observed two delightful picnic spots, both to the left of the trail and at the base of short steep rises. I came upon the first a short distance from the Greenpicker-Stewart junction, a gently sloping and small green meadow partly shaded by large Douglas firs and bay trees to the left of the trail at the base of the first abrupt climb (50 yards up 100-150 vertical feet). The second picnic spot came 10-15 minutes of steady hiking later. It was 40 feet to the left of a slightly longer and steeper rise at 1000 feet above sea level on the topographical map. The second spot, like the first, was small, intimate, and partly shaded by large Douglas firs.

---

[1]Actually the Greenpicker Trail now turns west to Glen Camp at a point some 300 to 400 yards from the open meadow at Fir Top. However, the old Greenpicker Trail continues, from this junction, along the wooded ridge to Fir Top and is clearly discernable. Meanwhile, the revised (1983) Greenpicker Trail plunges through a deep conifer forest for about 1.5 miles to Glen Camp.

The Greenpicker Trail gradually leveled off, dipped up and down, and then swung into more open and level terrain.

The Greenpicker Trail turned southward along the wooded Inverness Ridge, for a short distance, until it turned sharply westward and downward[1] at a point marked with a trail sign. I continued straight ahead on the wooded ridge and on what is an unnamed trail for a few hundred yards before coming upon the broad open meadow know as Fir Top. At Fir Top my unnamed trail junctioned with the Stewart Trail coming up from Five Brooks to the east.

On this particular bright spring morning, with the warm air bringing out the sweet scent of pine, I followed the Stewart Trail which drops away immediately to the south of Fir Top.

Within a few hundred yards of my having departed from Fir Top on the Stewart Trail, I came upon its junction with the Ridge Trail coming in from left (southeast). The Ridge Trail crosses the Stewart Trail and continues northwestward for a few steps before junctioning with the Greenpicker Trail. The Stewart Trail continued a southward course for one mile, dropping 400 vertical feet in that distance. The trail then veered temporarily northwestward for 1/2 mile to a junction with the Glen Trail. At the junction the trail signs clearly pointed out the options. A right turn on the Glen Trail would have taken me 1.2 miles uphill to Glen Camp. But, headed for the sea, I turned left and southwest towards Wildcat Camp 1.2 miles away.

As I dropped westward on the Stewart Trail I became aware of a rising wind as the forest began giving way to open brush country. The air was clear, crisp, and cool. Occasionally I caught a glimpse of Drakes Bay and the Pacific Ocean. In .5 mile I came upon the junction of the Stewart Trail and the Coast Trail coming up from Wildcat Beach and joining the Stewart Trail in a northward turn towards Bear Valley. I continued straight ahead and downhill on the Coast Trail towards Wildcat Camp .7 mile ahead.

In five minutes I broke out into full view of the broad green meadow which marks Wildcat Camp some 400 feet below the trail. 500 yards of additional descent brought me out onto the sunlit meadow where the grass was sparkling in the noon sun and dancing in a sharp wind out of the northwest.

After a short lunch in a sheltered spot on the beach nearby I resumed my hike on the Coast Trail as it climbs steeply to the east for about 150 yards before turning southward. About 200 yards from Wildcat Camp the Coast Trail meets the Ocean-Lake Loop Trail which veers off to the right, passing to the west of Wildcat Lake 300 yards from the junction. The Ocean Lake Loop Trail continues in open country and offers a fine view of the sea. In about 1/2 mile Ocean-Lake is reached. Passing onward (southward) one comes upon a small footpath branching off the Ocean-Lake Loop Trail and descending along a small cascade to the beach immediately north of Alamere Falls (a good way to reach the falls for a side trip). This footpath is but a few yards from Ocean-Lake.

On this day I chose to move along the winding and open Coast Trail towards beautiful Pelican Lake (two miles from Wildcat Camp and off the trail) to the southern junction with the Ocean-Lake Loop Trail. Some 500 yards beyond the southern junction with the Ocean-Lake Loop Trail the Coast Trail crosses Alamere Creek, climbs up some 130 vertical feet over some 250 to 300 yards, and connects with a small footpath, somewhat overgrown, which circumvents much of the western shore of Pelican Lake. From the junction with the footpath, Coast Trail climbs gradually for about 150 feet over 700 yards. Then the trail begins to level off and turn away from Pelican Lake below. At this point one can take a short diversion to discover a magnificent panorama of Pelican Lake, much of the Drakes Bay coastline and Point Reyes. Follow an overgrown footpath through coyote brush for 250 to 300 yards to an open hill south of your departure point on the Coast Trail. From the hill one of the finest and most unique views in Point Reyes National Seashore can be enjoyed. But watch out for poison oak along the first 50-60 yards of the footpath.

Back on the Coast Trail, I found myself moving into the forest, for some 500 yards, to the north shore of Bass Lake.[2] Here picnickers had launched a plastic raft and were busily paddling across the lake. Pelican and Bass Lakes are about 3/4 mile in circumference each. Wildcat and Ocean Lakes are about 1/2 mile in circumference, but marshy. Crystal Lake is 1/2 mile northeast of Pelican Lake and can be reached by a small trail branching off to the left of the Coast Trail about half way between Pelican and Bass Lakes.

3/4 mile beyond Bass Lake, I found myself at the junction of the Coast Trail and the Lake Ranch Trail. At the junction, at a point where nine large fir trees are to be seen to the right or west of the Coast Trail, the old Lake Ranch homestead stood.

The Lake Ranch Trail climbs for 650' over three miles. I found an increasingly fine view as I climbed through open terrain, the brush

---

[2]Bass Lake is a 12 acre springfed lake approximately 150 feet deep. Although you won't find bass, you can anticipate seeing such wild life as ducks and deer. The water temperature of around 58 to 60 degrees makes it appealing for swimming. No camping is allowed.

covered western slope of the Inverness Ridge. White and purple bush lupines brightened the steady climb which, in two miles from the junction with the Coast Trail, began leading into the deep forest of the Inverness Ridge. By the time I was 1/2 mile from Mud Lake I was well into the forest with Drakes Bay entirely hidden by towering and thick Douglas fir.

A half mile beyond Mud Lake and in gently rolling but generally level terrain, I came to the junction of the Lake Ranch Trail, Ridge Trail, and Bolema Trail. With the sun already dropping on the western horizon, I took the shorter route back to Five Brooks by way of the Bolema Trail, and, after one mile, the Olema Valley Trail, a total distance of 2-3 miles from the 3-way trail junction[3]. My route, mostly wooded, was marked by forget-me-nots, just beginning to come up along the edge of the trail. The road "switched-back" its way down the eastern slope of the Inverness Ridge, and at a few points I discovered a fine view up the Olema Valley, through which runs the rift zone of the San Andreas Earthquake fault, and of portions of the ridges on either side of the valley. In contrast to this wooded western slope of the rift zone-Olema Valley, the eastern slope (culminating in the Bolinas Ridge) is open and generally unwooded in its lower portion.

I came upon the small pond at the Five Brooks Trailhead as the sinking sun cast long shadows across the meadows. How I never tire of this magnificent land.

---

[3] 2.3 miles from the Coast Trail the Lake Ranch Trail junctions with the Crystal Lake Trail coming up from Crystal Lake 3.3 miles to the west. A beautiful route!

On the Ridge Trail.

CHAPTER 9

The Palomarin — Lake Ranch Ridge Trails Loop

Palomarian Trailhead — Lake Ranch site — Lake Ranch Trail — Mud Lake — Ridge Trail/Bolema Trail/Lake Ranch Trail junction — Ridge Trail — Mesa Road — Palomarin Trailhead

10 – 11 miles — Involves 1100 vertical feet of climbing and descending.
Moderate

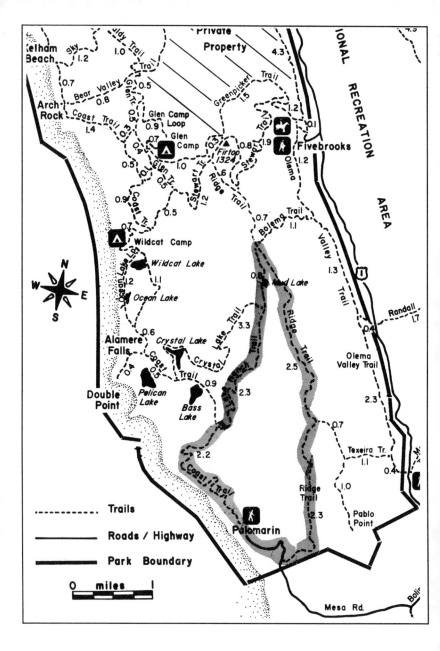

We started up on a calm spring morning, as a fog was lifting, from Palomarin Trailhead. Starting out on the Coast Trail we were soon winding along an open coastal shelf. Mustard, ice plant, golden poppies, iris, buttercups, cowsnips, monkey flower, wild rose, lupines, morning glory, daffodils, and poison oak all made themselves evident as the bright sunlight burned away the last traces of fog. A northwest wind, typical for spring afternoons, began to set the tall grass to dancing. In less than a mile the trail turned away from the coast and gradually took up northerly and upward directions to the junction with the Lake Ranch Trail. We considered going on along the Coast Trail to one of the lakes — Bass, Crystal, or Pelican — for lunch, something which can be easily worked in with this particular hike, but such a diversion would have lengthened our hike by two or three miles and we had started late from Palomarin.

Going up the Lake Ranch Trail, we found the sides of the trail alive with all the wildflowers previously mentioned plus Indian paint brush and thistle. Sage and manzanita began to make their appearance. The air, which had been quite cool right along the Coast Trail from Palomarin to the junction with the Lake Ranch Trail, was now warmer, having been heated by the inland hills through which we were now passing.

In the 1/2 mile beyond Mud Lake the Lake Ranch Trail meets the Bolema Trail and the Ridge Trail in the deep fir forest. We turned southeast and started out on the Ridge Trail.

The Ridge Trail had been winding for slightly over 1 1/2 miles southeastward from its northern terminus at "Fir Top" when it reached this junction with the Bolema and Lake Ranch Trails. Throughout these 1.6 miles the trail is shaded by giant Douglas firs and fringed, occasionally, by tiny patches of green meadow, ferns, and huckleberry. From the junction on towards Palomarin, the southern terminus of the trail, the Ridge Trail continues to be shaded by the abundant firs. However, I soon came upon evidence of indiscriminate logging — probably from an earlier time by 10 or 15 years. Numerous stumps between 10 and 24 inches in diameter were scattered amid coyote brush and manzanita. A few mature firs remained, but the young firs, 10 to 20 feet in height, were more numerous.

The Ridge Trail rolled gently up and down. The fluctuations in altitude were never more than 50 to 100 feet and were always gradual. Occasionally we came upon fine views of the Bolinas Ridge across the Olema Valley to the east. But to the west, the ocean was effectively blocked from view by the forest because most of the timber cutting had taken place on the east side of the Ridge Trail. California lilac bushes were in bloom in the areas where the cutting had been more widespread as were blackberry vines. 2.5 miles from the Bolema — Lake Ranch — Ridge trails junction we came upon another junction. Branching off to the left was the Texeria Trail to Pablo Point (100 yards north of this junction and to the east of the trail some 50 yards a beautiful green meadow spread beneath tall virgin firs. A fine place to escape the heat). Pablo Point is 1.8 miles from this junction. If one continues on the Ridge Trail it will be 2.3 miles to Mesa Road and another 1.2 miles to Palomarin Trailhead.

We kept on the Ridge Trail which began immediately to drop. In about a 1/2 mile from the junction we broke out onto a high and open hill commanding a magnificent view of Bolinas Lagoon, Stinson Beach, the Bolinas Ridge, the western shoulder of Mount Tamalpais, and San Francisco west of Twin Peaks. The land mass around Sharp Park and Pacifica jetted prominently into the sea and could easily have been mistaken for an island by someone who was ignorant of the San Francisco Bay Area's geography.

The remainder of the route along the Ridge Trail involved a steady drop southward for 100-150 yards then an abrupt westward turn over open hills just coming alive with wildflowers — bluegrass, lupines, Indian paint brush, and iris. In one mile from the scenic picnic spot just behind us the trail dropped about 600-700 vertical feet to Mesa Road, the roadway which connects Bolinas to the Palomarin Trailhead. Once on Mesa Road we had a 1.2 mile winding trek which we covered very quickly in order to avoid the exposure to dust stirred up by autos on the Mesa Road.

On the last mile along Mesa Road we passed the Point Reyes Bird Observatory,[1] which is dedicated to the preservation of bird life within the National Seashore area. At the observatory are situated both a small museum and a bird watchers' lookout.

Moving on, we came to the Palomarin parking lot as both the nearby grass and distant sea danced wildly in the typical springtime wind.

---

[1]For additional information, refer to Chapter 16.

Dairy cattle at the mouth of Abbotts Lagoon.

CHAPTER 10

The Point Reyes Beach Hike

Point Reyes Beach South —
Point Reyes Beach North —
Abbotts Lagoon — Kehoe Beach —
return to Point Reyes.

14 – 15 miles
Moderate — Level hiking on beach sand.

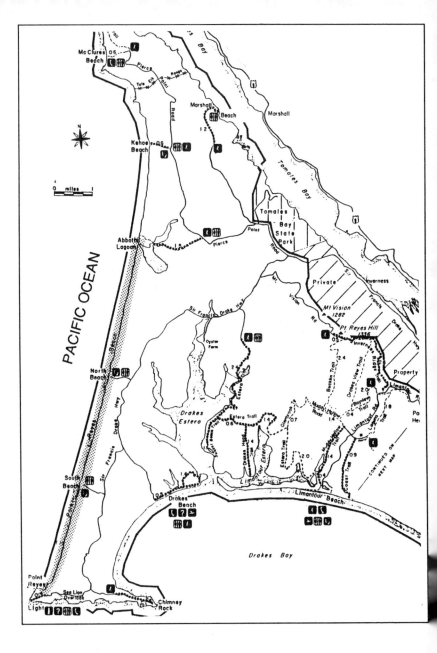

G oing up Point Reyes Beach from the point itself to McClures Beach is a unique experience. We hiked from the sandy beach just north and down a sandy hill from the Sir Francis Drake Highway as it comes to within 500 yards of the Point Reyes Lighthouse. Our descent to the beach, 400-450 vertical feet below, took us down a gentle and sandy slope. The route was strictly cross country so one should use a topographical map and do a little reconoitering to find the easiest way down to the beach.

Once on the beach, we turned northward and began a long and somewhat monotonous sandy hike towards Abbotts Lagoon. Varied configurations of driftwood were scattered all along the beach some 100 to 150 feet back from the water. Many of the pieces were huge logs which may have originated in any one of the many large rivers of northern California and Oregon, only to be cast up by heavy storms. Behind the driftwood a low ridge of dunes stretched endlessly northwards towards McClures Beach, vaguely visible on the northern horizon. The dunes stretched inland for a few hundred yards. Clumps of dune grass protruded up through the fine granules of white sand. It was too early in the year for yellow lupines, but in spring a few clumps may be found farther inland between the first ridge of dunes and the Sir Francis Drake Highway.

2.5 miles up the beach we came upon what is now Point Reyes Beach South, a stretch of beach accessible by auto since the Park Service has built a road less than a mile in length linking Sir Francis Drake Highway with Point Reyes Beach. Point Reyes Beach South is not distinct from the beach anywhere on this long expanse of ocean front. In fact, the only truly distinctive landmark along the entire route from Point Reyes itself to McClures Beach is Abbotts Lagoon, 8.5 miles from where we started our great sand trek.

In another two miles we came upon the beach now known as Point Reyes Beach North. Today the National Park Service maintains a beach access facility — parking lot, rest rooms, bulletin board, garbage cans, and ranger patrol.

I was taken with the steep angle with which the beach dropped off into the sea and with the power of the breakers on what was a windless day. The surf was in constant turmoil. The roar of crashing breakers, punctuated by the high pitched swish of seawater churning onto the sand close to our feet, was constant.

8-9 miles from our starting point at the northern base of the northern cliffs of Point Reyes itself we came upon Abbotts Lagoon. The Lagoon is 4-5 miles in circumference. Its brackish water serves as a stop over spot for migrating birds. The Lagoon[1] is surrounded by broad dunes that suggest an ancient inlet or bay for the eastern end of the lagoon is over a mile inland from the sea. We had wondered if the lagoon was connected with the sea, but found that a low sandbar separated the two. A storm, however, could easily pour ocean water over the sandbar and into the lagoon.

On the return hike from Abbotts Lagoon to Point Reyes we loitered to examine the driftwood, eat dinner, and take a few pictures. Miles before reaching Point Reyes and our sandy hill climb to the autos, we were overtaken by darkness. The night was moonless but a million stars glittered overhead to give just enough light to enable us to see our way down the beach. We couldn't see the breakers, but we could hear them pounding constantly. The lighthouse at

---

[1]The Lagoon is immediately accessible from the Pierce Point Road, off of which the National Park Service maintains a small trailhead.

Point Reyes was not visible, nor was there any man-made light to be seen anywhere. The night air was still and the monotony of crashing breakers was broken only by the occasional screech of an unseen seagull. The faint silhouette of Point Reyes gradually became more and more distinct indicating that we

Point Reyes Beach — view from Kehoe Beach to Point Reyes.

were making progress towards our destination. For over two hours we hiked in almost total darkness except for the starlight above.

We reached the base of our sandy hill unexpectedly because we could not see it until we were actually on it. There were two flashlights in a party of 15, and we had purposely saved them for this last part of the hike. With their help we struggled up the sandy hill to our autos, waiting in the darkness on the shoulder of the Sir Francis Drake Highway. Far out to sea a ship light flashed periodically as we took a last look at the black mass of land and sea. And from somewhere in that vast and dark mass we could hear, more distant now but as incessant as ever, the eternal crash of breakers on Point Reyes Beach.

On Kelum Beach.

CHAPTER 11

Other Hikes in Point Reyes National Seashore

Palomarin Trailhead to Bear Valley Trailhead (13.9 miles) — Five Brooks Trailhead to Bear Valley Trailhead (11.8 miles) — Limantour Beach to Palomarin Trailhead (15.1 miles) — Bear Valley Trailhead to Limantour Beach (8.5 miles) — Bayview-Muddy Hollow (5.0 miles) — Rift Zone Trail (4.4 miles) — Earthquake Trail (.7 mile).

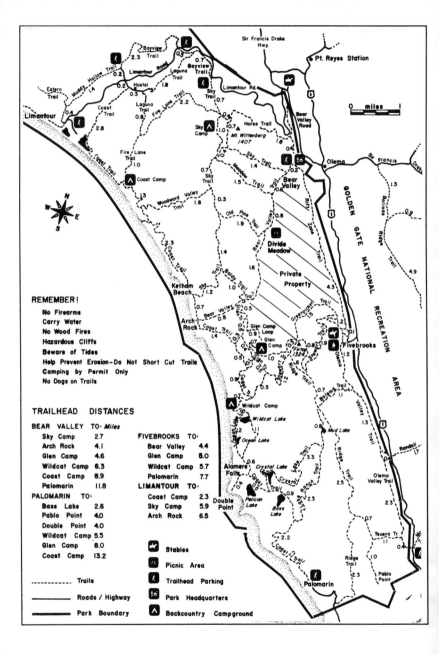

Sir Francis Drake Hwy.

Pt. Reyes Station

Bayview Trail 2.3

Bayview Trail 0.2

Muddy Hollow Trail

Limantour Rd. 1.4

Estero Trail

Hostel 0.3

Laguna Trail 1.8

Sky Trail 0.7

Limantour Rd.

Bear Valley Road

0 miles 1

Coast Trail 2.8

Laguna Trail 0.8

Fire Lane Trail 2.2

Sky Camp

Horse Trail 0.7 1.0

Mt. Wittenberg 1407

1.8 0.4

Olema

Sir Francis

Limantour 0.4

Fire Lane Trail 1.0

0.7 Sky Trail

Meadow 1.4

Sky Trail 1.5

Trail

Bear Valley

1.3

Coast Camp

Woodward Valley Trail 1.8

0.3

GOLDEN GATE NATIONAL

0.8

Bolinas

0.9

2.3

Old Pine Trail 1.9

Bear Valley Trail

Divide Meadow

Ridge Trail 4.9

Coast Trail

1.4

1.6

Private Property

Kelham Beach

Sky Trail 1.2 1.0

Baldy Trail

4.3

Greenpicker Trail 1.5

1.2 0.1

REMEMBER!

No Firearms
Carry Water
No Wood Fires
Hazardous Cliffs
Beware of Tides
Help Prevent Erosion-Do Not Short Cut Trails
Camping by Permit Only
No Dogs on Trails

0.7

Arch Rock

0.6

Bear Valley Trail

Coast Trail 1.4

0.5

Glen Camp Loop 0.9

Glen Camp 1.0

Fire 1.324

0.8 1.9

Olema

Fivebrooks

1.2

1.0

0.9

0.7

Bolinas Trail 1.1

0.5

RECREATION

TRAILHEAD DISTANCES

BEAR VALLEY TO: Miles
Sky Camp   2.7
Arch Rock   4.1
Glen Camp   4.6
Wildcat Camp   6.3
Coast Camp   8.9
Palomarin   11.8

PALOMARIN TO:
Bass Lake   2.6
Pablo Point   4.0
Double Point   4.0
Wildcat Camp   5.5
Glen Camp   8.0
Coast Camp   13.2

FIVEBROOKS TO:
Bear Valley   4.4
Glen Camp   5.0
Wildcat Camp   5.7
Palomarin   7.7

LIMANTOUR TO:
Coast Camp   2.3
Sky Camp   5.9
Arch Rock   6.5

Wildcat Camp

Wildcat Lake

1.2 1.1

Ocean Lake

0.8 Mud Lake

1.3

2.5

2.3

Alamere Falls 0.6

Crystal Lake

3.3

0.9

Bass Lake

0.7

Olema Valley Trail

Randall 1.7

2.3

Pelican Lake

0.4

Coast Trail

Double Point

2.2

Teixeira Tr. 1.1

1.0

0.4

Ridge Trail

1.2 2.3

Palomarin

Pablo Point

Stables

Picnic Area

Trailhead Parking

Park Headquarters

Backcountry Campground

AREA

N W E S

Fire Lane Trail

Coast Trail

Bear Valley Trail

Bolinas Ridge Trail

.... Trails
─────── Roads / Highway
━━━━━━ Park Boundary

PALOMARIN TRAILHEAD to BEAR VALLEY TRAILHEAD

This hike can be taken in reverse. It's just as beautiful one way as the other. Arbitrarily, I'll start you at Palomarin. Proceed on the Coast Trail to the Lake Ranch Trail junction (2.2 miles), continue on the Coast Trail past Bass Lake, Pelican Lake, Ocean Lake, and Wildcat Lake to Wildcat camp (5.4 miles from Palomarin). From Wildcat Camp go up the Coast Trail to Miller Point (8.5 miles from Palomarin Trailhead). From Miller Point pick up the Bear Valley Trail and hike on to Bear Valley Trailhead 4.4 miles from Miller Point. Total distance 13.9 miles. *Moderate. About 1200 feet of climbing and descending.*

FIVE BROOKS TRAILHEAD to BEAR VALLEY TRAILHEAD

Start at Five Brooks and go up the Stewart Trail or Stewart and Greenpicker Trails to Fir Top (3 miles from Five Brooks via Stewart Trail). Proceed west on Stewart Trail to the junction with the Glen Trail (5.2 miles from Five Brooks). Continue down the Stewart Trail to its junction with the Coast Trail (5.8 miles from Five Brooks via Stewart Trail). Go up the Coast Trail to its junction with the small unnamed trail connecting it with the Glen Trail (north end) about 1.7 miles from Wildcat Camp. On the Glen Trail, continue first level, then downhill and northward to the junction with the Bear Valley Trail (8.6 miles from Five Brooks). Proceed to Olema Trailhead (3.2 miles). Total distance 11.8 miles. *Moderate. A shorter route between these two trailheads (9 miles) can be put together.*

LIMANTOUR BEACH (or Point Reyes Hostel) to
PALOMARIN TRAILHEAD

Proceed on Coast Trail to Coast Camp (3 miles from Point Reyes Hostel). Continue south on Coast Trail to junction with Woodward Valley Trail (4.3 miles from the Hostel). Continue south to the Kellum Beach (6.5 miles from the Hostel) and to Miller Point at the Arch Rock overlook (7.3 miles from the Hostel). Climb up on the Coast Trail to its connection with the Glen Trail (1.4 miles from Miller Point) and follow the Coast Trail down to Wildcat Beach (3 miles from Miller Point). From Wildcat Beach take the Coast Trail southward on past Wildcat Lake, Ocean Lake, Pelican Lake, and Bass Lake to the junction with the Lake Ranch Trail (13 miles from the Hostel). Continue on the Coast Trail to Palomarin two miles ahead. Total distance 15 miles. *Moderate-strenuous. About 1000 feet of up and down hill hiking is involved.*

BEAR VALLEY TRAILHEAD to the POINT REYES HOSTEL
(or Limantour Beach)

Proceed down the Bear Valley Trail to the junction with Sky Trail (200-250 yards from Bear Valley Trailhead). Go up the Sky Trail to Mount Wittenberg (1.8 miles from Bear Valley Trailhead). Drop down to the Sky Trail from Mount Wittenberg (.2 miles). Follow the Sky Trail to its junction with the Fire Lane (3 miles from Bear Valley Trailhead). Follow the Fire Lane (described in detail in Chapter 4) down to Coast Camp and the Coast Trail. Proceed along the Coast Trail to the Hostel (8.5 miles from Bear Valley Trailhead). Total distance 8.5 miles. For a more direct route to the Hostel take the

Laguna Trail off the Fire Lane (2.2 miles from the junction of the Fire Lane and Sky Trail) and follow it (.8 mile) to the Hostel. *Easy except for 1200' climb to top of Mount Wittenberg.*

BAYVIEW-MUDDY HOLLOW HIKE

Have someone who is heading down the Limantour Road to Limantour Beach (the Park Service maintains the road and a parking lot near the beach) drop you off at the Bayview Trailhead at the crest of the Limantour Road where it crosses the Olema Ridge. The Bayview Trail is well surrounded, at its outset, by the unique Bishop pine, lilac bushes, and coyote brush.

After about a mile of gentle down hill walking one breaks out into semi-open hills with the first view of Drakes Bay. From then on the trail drops more sleeply over increasingly open hills to the Muddy Hollow Trailhead about 3 miles from the Bayview Trailhead. The Muddy Hollow Trail is a naturalist's delight as it moves along a generally straight and level course to the sea 1.75 miles from the Trailhead. In evidence are groves of alders, blackberry bushes, Queen Anne's lace, cowslips, blue grass, Indian paint brush, cattails, blue lupine, yellow monkey flower, orange monkey flower and wild oats. From Muddy Hollow, just behind the dunes of Limantour Beach, one can go on a few hundred yards to the Limantour parking lot to meet his or her ride. *A pleasant down hill 5 mile saunter with plant and animal life to look at.*

THE RIFT ZONE TRAIL

The Rift Zone Trail connects Five Brooks Trailhead with the Bear Valley Trailhead at Olema. The trail moves through level terrain and is generally parallel to the San Andreas Earthquake faultline. A sophisticated viewer can see evidence of the faultline while hiking from Five Brooks Trailhead to the Bear Valley Trailhead. In fact, the Rift Zone Trail crosses the earthquake fault some 200 yards south of the Bear Valley Trailhead parking lot.

The Rift Zone Trail, which crosses the Vedanta Religious Retreat, passes through green meadows (expect to see cattle grazing in the first mile south of bear Valley Trailhead), through forests of fir, madrone, oak, and alder, and emerges once again into open meadows. This is a gentle hike and one which is especially suited for families with small children. Transportation is the only problem, since one starts at one trailhead and finishes at another. Explore having someone pick you up. This is particularly desirable if one is making this hike with small children.

For anyone, this is a beautifully pastoral region which should be hiked very leisurely to be enjoyed. *Total distance 4.4 miles. Easy.*

THE EARTHQUAKE TRAIL

An exciting feature of Point Reyes National Seashore is the presence of the San Andreas earthquake faultline. The earthquake faultline comes into Marin County and the National Seashore from under the Pacific Ocean off the mouth of Tomales Bay. It runs under Tomales Bay, then overland through the Park Headquarters at Olema, and down the Olema Valley to the sea just off Stinson Beach.

The linear Tomales Bay gives clear indication of the direction of the faultline. At the Park Headquarters there are cypress trees, just opposite (northward) the Visitor Center, which were displaced by the 1906 earthquake. The faultline runs smack under the road from which you will be turning into the Visitor Center.

Just past the Visitor Center and Headquarters is the parking area known as Bear Valley Trailhead. The Earthquake Trail, a .7 mile loop walk which is a kind of self-guided tour of various points of geologic and historic interest along the fault line, begins at the southeast edge of the unpaved parking area diagonally across from the Visitor Center. The trail begins in front of a wooden restroom facility. Don't miss an old fence, which was displaced some 18 feet in 1906 by the lateral shifting of the earth's surface. Still standing today, it is a testimonial to the colossal power of earthquakes.

At the location of the displaced fence, one can look towards the blacksmith's shop next to the Visitor Center and see a line of blue stakes which have been positioned to mark the actual faultline. *A .7 mile walk.*

A FINAL NOTE

Marked trails are those whose starting point and junctions with other trails are marked with a trail sign which at least tells the hiker the name of the trail he or she is about to follow. The markers usually include, also, an indication of the distance to the next junction and/or location. If you should get lost, or firmly believe you are lost, head for any Trailhead: Bear Valley, Palomarin, Five Brooks, Limantour, Estero Trail, Muddy Hollow, McClures, Tomales Point, Bayview. At any of these trailheads you will find a parking lot and, most likely, other hikers and automobiles. At the Bear Valley Trailhead you will find permanent ranger headquarters and a public phone (should you arrive after the Visitor Center closes at 5 p.m.).

If by some *remote* chance you get lost and are caught by darkness without flashlight, stay where you are until first light. Dress warmly, stay under trees and away from the open meadows or beach where it will be colder. The only thing which can hurt you under such circumstances is panic. Exposure is not a problem for anyone stuck overnight so long as one stays calm, dry and out of any wind.

A raincoat or pancho should be taken if there is the slightest possibility of a rainstorm. Even on warm days, because the temperature can change, one should always carry a heavy sweater or parka in a knapsack. If you are forced to spend the night, *do not start a fire.* It could easily get away from you and greatly complicate matters. Stay among the trees and try to sleep. When you walk out the next morning, tell a ranger you're out and okay just in case it's your friends and/or family who panicked. The main thing is — you didn't!

Keyhole at northern end of Secret Beach.

In this trail guide I have attempted to describe the major trails and points of natural and aesthetic interest in Point Reyes National Seashore. Any of these can be modified to suit the interest of the particular hiker.

I have not suggested all of the hikes that one can take in Point Reyes National Seashore. For me to list every possible hike would be to take much of the joy and adventure out of letting one put one's own hike plan together. So the hiker who wishes to put together his or her own particular hike plan can use this guide plus any combination of maps, including the ones in this guide, to do just that.

Stretching at Divide Meadow.

CHAPTER 12

Conditioning For Trailhiking

At the western end of the Bear Valley Trail.

Hiking is a physical activity which can be enjoyed for its own sake and/or the aesthetic pleasures found in the places where only hikers can go. There is little skill associated with the physical act of hiking, for hiking is nothing more than walking.

But hiking can become strenuous, relative to the individual, when it involves long uphills, long downhills, or long levels. By my definition, "strenuous" activity is activity which places a strain on any or all parts of the body.

Uphill hiking (especially with heavy pack and/or at high altitude) is strenuous for the average person. The most effective training for uphill hiking/backpacking for me is running. Running conditions one's legs, just as, or even more important for uphill hiking/ backpacking, it conditions the cardio-vascular system.

From running I learned the three essential things one must know for uphill hiking and backpacking: pace, rhythmic breathing, and overbreathing. Pace means you walk sufficiently slowly so that your breathing is comfortable, so that you are not gasping, so that you are not forced to stop, periodically, to catch your breath. It means walking at a pace sufficiently slow that your muscles do not ache. Pacing does not mean that your breathing rate is the same as it is sitting down reading. It does not mean that you need to breathe only through your nose, as some people insist. Pace means that your walking rhythm is slow enough so that, while breathing more heavily than in a resting posture, you are yet able to keep the pace without need to stop due to breathlessness or aching muscles.

Rhythmic breathing, synchronized to one's walking pace, guarantees a continual and uniform oxygen supply while exerting.

Tomales Bay from near the Tomales Point Trail.

Rhythmic breathing means that the time interval between breaths is the same, that the amount of time consumed in taking in and letting out air is the same.

Overbreathing, sometimes referred to as "hyperventilating," means that one consciously and deliberately breathes a little more deeply than seems necessary while moving uphill. Too much overbreathing — too fast and/or too deep — results in dizziness. Experimentation will quickly help a person find his or her own optimum degree of overbreathing and his or her own tempo of breathing. You may find that you will tend to "shift gears" in overbreathing and rhythmic breathing — a little faster and a little deeper for higher altitudes and/or heavier pack and/or steeper terrain and/or untrailed terrain. That is, you learn to breathe a little more deeply and at a slightly faster tempo if there is more exertion. And you learn, should you get dizzy, that you are breathing too fast and/or too deeply for the degree of exertion. In time it really becomes automatic, but one has to be patient and experiment.

Hiking on level or downhill terrain does not require "wind." A running program will strengthen leg, back, and stomach muscles, but hiking itself is probably the best conditioner for level or downhill hiking. However, most of us who work from Monday through Friday do not always have time to take a long training hike two to four times during the week. Running, which takes but 15-30 minutes to get a good workout, can, then, have an advantage over hiking as a training technique.

Hiking does place more strain on joints than muscles. A long hike places considerable strain on one's feet, toes, arches and heels, so it is important to build up gradually to the point where one can handle a given distance without placing undue strain on joints and feet. Proper footgear is essential.

Hikers descending the foot trail leading from Coast Trail to Sculptured Beach.

CHAPTER 13

Equipment and Clothing for Hiking in Point Reyes National Seashore

Pelican Lake from 150 yards off the Coast Trail at the latter's junction with the Crystal Lake Trail.

H iking equipment and clothing for hiking in Point Reyes National Seashore differs hardly at all from hiking equipment and clothing anywhere whether one is out for a day or for three or four days.

Footgear is probably the most important item of equipment since most people hike only for the day in Point Reyes and do not encumber themselves with much more than knapsack, lunch, water bottle, and camera. For trailhiking in a place like Point Reyes National Seashore heavy boots are unnecessary. A lightweight trail boot, properly fitted and properly cared for between hikes is all one needs. Any lightweight (no heavier than 3 1/2 pounds) trail shoe or hiking boot, such as those found at mountaineering stores is especially recommended. Trail boots made partly of Gore-tex are light and comfortable. A sturdy pair of tennis shoes or running shoes are just as good unless one has weak ankles. Tennis shoes or running shoes should have good arch support and good heel support. Do not hike in lightweight marathon running shoes. They're too thin, lack sufficient arch support, and have virtually no heel support. Some individuals can manage with these or any inadequate footgear (I've seen a few going barefooted on the trail!), but for the sometime or beginning hiker, no!

A RECOMMENDED EQUIPMENT LIST FOR A DAY HIKE IN POINT REYES NATIONAL SEASHORE:

---

1. comfortable trail boots or sturdy tennis shoes, with good heel and arch support

2. 2 pairs of cotton socks or light weight wool socks for trail shoes or hiking boots

3. knapsack with plenty of side pockets

4. hiking shorts (optional)

5. full length trousers (I take both hiking shorts and a pair of long trousers in case the day grows colder or there is poison oak

6. dark glasses, especially if you are going on the beach

7. cotton shirt or blouse

8. wool sweater and windbreaker with hood, or down parka with hood

9. Swiss Army knife

10. wool cap (optional – good in winter or on windy beaches)

11. First Aid kit (light and simple)

12. camera equipment (optional, but highly recommended)

13. notebook and pencil

14. topographical map

15. trail map

16. extra toilet paper

17. 1 quart plastic water bottle filled before you leave a trailhead

18. sponge rubber heel lifts (eases the stress placed on the heels by the constant pounding action during the hike)

19. sun hat (optional, except for those who burn easily)

20. sunburn cream (especially in summer and spring)

21. *Exploring Point Reyes—A Guide to Point Reyes National Seashore*

22. binoculars (optional, but essential for close up views of wildlife)

23. raingear—jacket and pants recommended, pancho OK, umbrella only for short windless hikes. Take raingear if there is the slightest chance of rain.

RECOMMENDED EQUIPMENT LIST FOR OVERNIGHT EXCURSIONS TO POINT REYES NATIONAL SEASHORE:

1. all items recommended for day hikes, except that a pack frame and bag are preferable, in my opinion, to a knapsack

2. sleeping bag -- Coast Camp and Wildcat Camp are especially damp. The cold nightime air and high humidity mean dew. A fiberfill bag is somewhat preferable to a down bag in these circumstances. Yet down works satisfactorily, especially if one sleeps inside a lightweight tent. If one doesn't have any kind of tent, then it is better to sleep under trees (plenty at Glen Camp and at Sky Camp, but hardly any at Coast or Wildcat Camp). However, if it's a very foggy night, the trees will drip so it is my recommendation that one sleep inside a tent or tube tent.

3. tent or tube tent — I strongly suggest that the tube tent be erected by first running it through a nylon cord, both ends of which are tied to nearby trees or firmly established stakes. A lightweight camping tent is infinitely preferable to a tube tent, but the latter is much cheaper.

4. stove (no cooking fires except hot coals/briquets used in on-site facilities are allowed in the Seashore area) — A Bluett stove is light and good for easy-to-cook meals involving a short time use of fuel. An Optimus 111B or 8R stove cook hotter, but the 111B is much heavier than the Bluett or 8R. The Bluett burns butane fuel in easy to attach, easy to remove canisters. The Optimus 8R and 111B burn white gasoline, which means that you will need to carry a fuel container if staying for more than one night. Both the Coleman Peak 1 stove and the MSR Firefly are light and efficient. The Svea stove is lightweight and burns over an hour on a tank of fuel.

5. ensolite or foam pad — 4' length of 1/2" x 3/4" pad to insulate you from the hard ground at night.

6. ground cloth — an 8' x 3' plastic ground cloth is recommended only if you aren't going with tent or tube tent.

7. *lightweight* cooking pots, griddles, fry pans adequate to the cooking needs at hand — Stirring spoons, ladles, spatulas as needed.

8. cup, spoon, fork, plate — all lightweight

9. scouring pad and biodegradable soap

10. matches — Carried in a plastic bag, sealed.

11. flashlight — Disengage the batteries for travel on the trail, lest you have a dead battery upon reaching camp.

12. food — Planned for economy of space and weight.

Baytree arches.

At Drakes Beach.

CHAPTER 14

Maps — Campsites
Point Reyes Hostel — Water
Poison Oak — Vegetation
Horses — Bicycles — Canoeing
Reptiles — Wildlife — Birds
Pets — Hunting & Fishing

Wildcat Camp and Beach from the Coast Trail.

MAPS

The hiker who is not familiar with Point Reyes National Seashore should carry a map. Hikers familiar with the area might find that a map will be handy when encountering something new and unexpected.

Topographical Maps. Four detailed maps, a 7 1/2 minute quadrangle series, are available: *Tomales, Drakes Bay, Inverness,* and *Double Point.* They all fit together to make a very sizeable map. However, one would seldom, if ever, need to put them all together on the trail. 2 5/8 inches represents one mile on the 7 minute series. Contour intervals are 40 feet. 1 5/8 inches represent 1 kilometer. You can practically pinpoint your own body on these maps. The topographical maps are all available at: The United States Geological Survey office 345 Middlefield Way, Menlo Park, California, 94025 (phone: map sales (415) 329-4390). Cost per map is $2.50. USGS Topographical maps are also available at Recreation Equipment Incorporated in Berkeley (corner of San Pablo and Gilman) and their other stores and at some other Bay Area mountaineering goods stores though supplies are limited.

Trail maps. The National Park Service has, at the Visitor Center, a fold-out map showing the entire seashore area with paved roads, visitor centers, trails, points of interest, and prominent landmarks. This map does not show topography.

The National Park Service has a large sign map of the entire Seashore area between Drakes Estero and Palomarin Trailhead. This map is placed at each of the three trailheads — Olema, Five Brooks, and Palomarin — and shows the names of most trails and distances between trail junctions. Trail distances from each trailhead to particular camps and points of interest are listed at the bottom of this map. The map does not show topography. The National Park Service has a smaller paper version of this map available at the Visitor Center at Bear Valley (Olema). As a last resort, a beginning hiker could always take a few minutes to make his own hand drawn copy of the maps placed at each of the three trailheads. The Park Service also has a handout trail map showing trails, named locations, and distances. Elevation is not shown. Also available at the Visitor Center are USGS topographical maps of the Point Reyes region.

Also of interest is an oblique-view pictorial land form map of Point Reyes National Seashore and the San Andreas fault by Dee Molenaar.

CAMPSITES

As of this writing there are four overnight campsites within the Seashore: Sky, Glen, Coast and Wildcat. These sites have wooden benches, crude restroom facilities, charcoal braziers with grills for each campsite, hitching rails for horses, and a water supply. The water supply is usually safe, but check with the ranger at the Visitor Center at Bear Valley before going ahead with your overnight plans (phone 415-663-1092 between 9:00 a.m. and 5:00 p.m.) or check in person. Wood fires are not permitted except on the beach, but check with the rangers. Beach fires must be away from swimming or grassy areas. Campsites must be reserved well in advance. Campsites cannot be reserved more than two months in advance. Reservations are taken from 9:00 a.m. until noon, Monday through Friday. Reservations for Saturdays and holidays are not held beyond 10 a.m.

• SKY CAMP — 2.7 mile hike from Bear Valley to campground. 12 sites; 1 group site. 1.2 mile hike from Sky Trailhead.

• GLEN CAMP — 4.6 mile hike from Bear Valley to campground. 12 sites; no group sites.

• COAST CAMP — 7 mile hike from Bear Valley to campground. 14 sites; 2 group sites. 2 mile walk from Limantour Beach parking lot.

• WILDCAT CAMP — 6.3 mile hike from Bear Valley to campground. 4 double campsites; 3 single sites. 5.5 miles from Palomarin Trailhead.

Each camp has a *four* night limit in park; any combination. On Friday and Saturday, the limit at Wildcat Camp is *four* nights. If you have secured a reservation for a particular campsite, check in at the Bear Valley (Olema) Visitor Center the morning of your overnight excursion and pick up a permit. There is a limit on the number of persons allowed at any of the four overnight camps, but be prepared to expect crowded conditions and lack of privacy.

Sleeping is not permitted on beaches.

Place your food in the food lockers provided. Raccoons and foxes are numerous and aggressive. Be sure to leave your campsite clean.

In periods of extreme fire hazard all overnight camping is suspended, so phone or contact the information office in person beforehand.

Or, should you prefer, a privately operated tent and trailer campground is 1/2 mile from Seashore Headquarters.

For additional information contact:

> Point Reyes National Seashore
> Point Reyes, California 94956 or phone: (415) 663-1092

POINT REYES AYH–HOSTEL

Point Reyes AYH-Hostel
P.O. Box 247, Point Reyes Station, CA 94956.
(415) 663-8811.
Office hours: 4:30–9:30 p.m. & 7:30–9:30 a.m.

Located in a secluded valley in Point Reyes National Seashore, this country hostel is a haven for hikers and a retreat for individuals or groups wanting a quick getaway from the city.

The Hostel. The Point Reyes AYH-Hostel is located two miles from Limantour Beach, and is accessible by car, foot, or bicycle.

Once a working ranch house, the Hostel offers all the amenities of a large vacation cabin, including a spacious, fully-equipped kitchen, hot showers, and an outdoor barbecue and patio. Hostelers share friendship, adventures and lively conservations in the two common rooms warmed by woodburning stoves. Up to 44 guests can enjoy moonlit nights sleeping soundly either in the main ranch house or the redwood bunkhouse. There is also a family room available in the main house.

Limited handicapped access. Please contact the hostel for complete information.

Rates:

$7.00 per person

Half price for children accompanied by parent.

Midweek discount offered to school groups during off-season.

Hosteling Customs. Hostelers around the world follow a few simple customs. Hostelers provide their own food, towels, soap and sleeping bag. Here, you are part of a community where everyone lends a hand after breakfast by doing a simple cleaning chore. It is this self-help system which allows hostels to be inexpensive and offer a friendly, cooperative spirit. Check-in hours are between 4:30 p.m. and 9:30 p.m.; the hostel is closed between 9:30 a.m. and 4:30 p.m. The use of intoxicants is not permitted on the premises, smoking is allowed outside the hostel only, and pets are not allowed. And, as in most hostels, travelers may stay a maximum of three days.

Groups. The Point Reyes AYH-Hostel is well suited to group use. In the past, hiking clubs, Girl Scout troops, photography seminars, bodywork seminars, bicycling groups, senior social clubs, religious retreats, youth outing groups, and many informal gatherings of families and friends have used the facility. A group of 20 or more can be guaranteed exclusive use of their own private redwood bunkhouse with large common room and fireplace. Please write or call as soon as you begin to make your plans.

Getting to the Hostel. From Highway 101 going north from San Francisco, take either Highway 1 through Stinson Beach (the winding, coastal route), or Sir Francis Drake Blvd. through San Anselmo and Samuel P. Taylor State Park. These two routes meet at the flashing stoplight in Olema. Immediately north of this junction turn left (west) at the sign for Point Reyes National Seashore. Proceed past Park Headquarters about 1.5 miles on Bear Valley Road to Limantour Road (marked by a sign for Limantour Natural Area.) Turn left here and follow this curving road for six miles. At the bottom of a steep grade there's a hostel sign; turn left. The hostel is just down the road on your left.

For bus information to the Bear Valley Visitor Center, 7 miles from the hostel, please call the hostel during open hours.

Reservations. We recommend making prepaid reservations at least 2-3 weeks in advance of your arrival at all times during the year. Deposit of first night's fee for all members of your party (please specify genders and children's ages) is required to secure a reservation. Please call the hostel during office hours (7:30-9:30 a.m. and 4:30-9:30 p.m.) to check availability. The family room may be reserved only if you bring a child aged 5 years or younger.

Cancellation & Refunds. At this hostel, a full refund will be given to individuals if a cancellation is made 2 weeks or more before arrival date. Attempts to move a reservation to a later date if requested at least one week prior to the original arrival date, will be made. Moving the arrival date will only be done once. No refunds can be made with less than two week's notice. For information about the cancellation and refund policy for groups, please contact the hostel.

WATER

Public health authorities have determined that it is unsafe to drink the water in the Point Reyes National Seashore area. It is especially advisable to avoid the water in summer and fall during a very dry year, and never to drink the water from lakes, or stream water which is not moving rapidly. I always carry fluid with me, and would advise you to do the same. One iodine tablet per four quarts of water will purify the water after allowing 20 minutes for dissolving

POISON OAK

There is lots of poison oak in the Point Reyes National Seashore area, particularily in forested regions. If hiking on established and maintained trails, there is less danger of coming in contact with poison oak, however. If going off-trail, other than along the beach, wear long trousers and a long-sleeved shirt. If you are extremely susceptible, avoid cross country travel and stay on marked trails. If you feel you have been exposed, wash the area of contact as soon as possible. Wash your clothes upon returning home. *Tecnu*, available in most drug stores, is the best known substance to wash poison oak oil off the skin, but don't use Tecnu on the trail. It is effective up to 12 hours after contact. Poison oak is systemic, which means you may break out in body locations other than the initial point of contact.

VEGETATION

ALONG THE BEACHES AND ESTEROS

grasses • marshy plants • bush • beach strawberry • lizard tail•
gum weed • coastal bush lupine (yellow) • sand verbena • wind
swept shrubs, particularly abundant coyote bush

INLAND GRASSLANDS

berry plants • poison oak • shrub • lupine • mustard • California
poppy • Indian paintbrush • Douglas iris • tidy tips• monkey
flower • morning glory • brodiaea • blue-eyed grass • suncups•
sneeze weed • goldfields • buttercups • blue eyes • blue grass

INVERNESS RIDGE AREA

Douglas fir • Bishop pine • California laurel • maple• tan oak •
coast live oak • madrone• alder   Pacific dogwood • Pacific
bayberry • California buckeye • western yew • manzanita •
poison oak • blue huckleberry • California coffeeberry • red and
blue elderberry •   salmonberry • thimbleberry •   nettle•
forget-me-nots • milkmaids • shooting stars • cow parsnip

Point Reyes has a number of endemic species and several rare and
endangered species of wild flowers. An example of a variety of a
wildflower found nowhere else is the yellow form of meadow foam.

Please remember, wildflowers must not be picked.

Flowers of Point Reyes National Seashore by Roxana S. Ferris (1970) is
an excellent field guide and reference. See appendix for additional
information.

HORSES

Horses are permitted in the Seashore area, with certain restrictions. A map is available which outlines designated trails on which horses are permitted. Horses may be rented at Five Brooks Stables (415) 663-1570 or Stewart's Horse Camp (415) 663-1362. Inquire about guides.

The Bear Valley Trail region, is open to the horseback rider as well as to hikers. About 70 miles of well-marked trails are available to riders. The same regulations that apply to saddle and pack animals in other national parks and recreation areas are in effect at Point Reyes.

Horses and other saddle or pack animals are permitted only on those trails or routes established for their use, except in those areas were cross-country travel is permitted by the Superintendent, such as along Santa Maria and Wildcat Beaches.

The use of horses or other saddle or pack animals upon the main roadways is prohibited except where such travel is necessary for entry to or egress from the trails, or is incidental to authorized travel.

In the interest of public safety and welfare, the Superintendent may require that saddle horse parties and/or pack trains shall be in charge of a licensed guide or other guide who meets qualifications which may be established by the Superintendent.

Riding horses or hitching horses in the campgrounds, in picnic areas, in the vicinity of eating or sleeping establishments or other areas of public gatherings *is prohibited*.

Riders shall slow their horses to a walk or slow trot when passing persons on foot or on bicycles.

At Point Reyes National Seashore these additional rules were established for the safety of all visitors:

Horses may **not** be ridden on the Bear Valley Trail, Meadow Trail, or Old Pine Trail on Saturdays, Sundays, or holidays.

Horses may not be ridden on the Woodward Valley Trail, the Estero Trail, Coast Trail between Arch Rock and Wildcat at any time.

Horses are not allowed on the Earthquake Trail at any time.

Horses may not be ridden on Drakes Beach.

The National Park Service asks that you not smoke while you are on a horse. Find a clear spot without flammable vegetation and dismount to smoke, being careful to break matches and extinguish all coals.

BICYCLES

Bicycles are prohibited within the wilderness areas. Bicyclists should check at one of the visitor centers about trail use and restrictions. Cyclists are a potential hazard to hikers in that some of them like to get up a full head of steam on the downhill sections of the Bear Valley Trail. Some of them don't give warning or, because they come around corners and turns too fast, are unable to give adequate warning. I have been narrowly missed by cyclists going 15-30 mph and I was actually struck, from behind, by a cyclist going about 10 mph. The greatest danger comes from those cyclists who are simply unaware or who just don't care as they race up from behind you. When cyclists are coming in a direction opposite to your own the danger is, of course, much less.

CANOEING

Abbots Lagoon is a choice place to canoe. It is also an excellent place to view migratory waterfowl. One can also canoe on Tomales Bay in calm seas. Launch at Heart's Desire Beach at Tomales Bay State Park off Pierce Point Road (see the Park Service fold out map available at the Visitor Center).

REPTILES

The western garter snake, gopher snake, and yellow-bellied racer are the snakes commonly found at Point Reyes National Seashore. I have never seen a rattlesnake, but am told they are at the Seashore. Lizards found include the southern alligator lizard, western fence lizard and western skink. Other reptiles found at the Seashore are the Pacific pond turtle and California newt.

WILDLIFE

There is a great variety of animal life in the Point Reyes National Seashore area. There are no bears in Bear Valley, in spite of the name. Thousands of Tule Elk were in the area before 1860. A small free-roaming herd has been reintroduced north of the old Pierce

Ranch. Tule Elk can be dangerous during rutting season. Heed the warnings of the signs.

Deer to be found at the seashore are black-tailed deer, the white fallow deer and the Indian axis dear.

Jack rabbits, pocket gophers, squirrels, badgers, skunks and brush rabbits abound.

Racoons and foxes can be pests at the campsites, and campers should protect their food by using the food lockers provided.

Also found inhabiting the Seashore are coyotes and bobcats, and mountain lions in the remote areas near Palomarin and the Tomales headlands.

An Annotated Checklist of Mammals of Point Reyes National Seashore by Gary M. Fellers and John Dell'Osso is an excellent reference on mammals. It is available at the Visitor Center.

See the appendix for more information.

BIRDS

More than 430 species of birds inhabit the Seashore at one time or another, much to the delight of birdwatchers.

Seabirds include gulls, cormorant, murres, pelicans, ducks, egrets and loons. Other birds include pigeons, hawks, kites, wrens, woodpeckers, turkey vultures, nut hatches, flycatchers and jays.

In the fall and winter, the wetlands of Limantour Estero are a haven for migrating shorebirds and waterfowl. Greater Yellowlegs, Green-winged Teals and Ring-necked Ducks can be seen.

During the winter, Hooded Mergansers and Wood Ducks may be spotted in the quiet seclusion of Fivebrooks Pond.

Migrating waterfowl may be seen at Drakes Estero.

See appendix for more information.

PETS

No pets are permitted on trails, in campgrounds or on designated beaches. Elsewhere they must be leashed. Certain beaches are open to dogs if leashed. These regulations do not apply to seeing-eye dogs.

HUNTING AND FISHING

Hunting is not permitted. The use of firearms, air guns, or weapons of any kind is prohibited. This also applies to fireworks.

A California fishing license is required of everyone 16 years and older who plans to fish.

See appendix for more information.

Just off the Rift Zone Trail near the Stewart Ranch.

CHAPTER 15

Interpretive
&
Special Programs

Female Tule elk.

Throughout the year, many different programs are offered by Park Rangers staffing the Seashore. Programs in the past have included spring wildflower walks; bird walks through marshes, grasslands, forests and ocean; Cultural history programs talking about the Coast Miwok Indians, early European explorers and current ranching tenants; geology of the peninsula and earthquakes; tidepooling programs that explore a different world that is seldom seen; the viewing of the annual California gray whale migration; and much more. Please pick up a free newspaper in any visitor center to find out what is currently being offered.

THE MONARCH BUTTERFLY

As days shorten and get cooler in the fall, the monarch butterflies throughout the western states begin flying to the Pacific Coast. They will gather in the same sites monarchs have used for generations. Hundreds of these dramatic black and orange butterflies have been known to cluster November through January in the eucalyptus trees at the Palomarin Trailhead. Look for them out sunning themselves or sipping nectar when the morning light warms the tree.

THE SPOTTED OWL

Hikers at dusk may be treated to the unusual "barking" calls of the rare spotted owl. Although endangered throughout most of its range, the spotted owl finds refuge in Marin County. Due to the county's unique heritage of use and protection, these denizens of the night are found in many of the deep, shady and cool canyons of the Seashore. If you are fortunate to find the day roost of these large nocturnal predators. approach quietly to observe and you may find them equally curious about you!

"ADOPT A TRAIL" PROGRAM

In an effort to combat budget cutbacks and restrictions which could jeopardize trail conditions at Point Reyes National Seashore, Park Superintendent John Sansing launched of an "Adopt a Trail" program.

It is hoped the program will encourage groups and organizations to *adopt* one of the park's trails, and provide maintenance at least two weekends a year. Work would include drainage and trail surface repair and water bar maintenance.

Tools, materials and general supervision will be provided.

For more information, call Point Reyes National Seashore Park Headquarters at (414) 663-8522.

POINT REYES FIELD SEMINARS

Point Reyes Field Seminars offer a wide variety of courses in natural history, environmental education and the arts. The courses are taught by recognized professionals, and many offer optional credit through Dominican College of San Rafael.

The program is a self-supporting non-profit activity, sponsored by the Point Reyes National Seashore Association in cooperation with Point Reyes National Seashore.

The seminars,which meet at Point Reyes National Seashore, are offered throughout the year.

For further information, or to be placed on the mailing list, write Seminar Coordinator, Point Feyes Field Seminars, Point Reyes, California 94956; or call (415) 663-1200.

GUIDED OUTINGS IN & AROUND
POINTS REYES NATIONAL SEASHORE

Sierra Pacific Educational Adventures
P.O. Box 1823
Vacaville, CA 95696
(707) 451-4453

Arnot Explorations
P.O. Box 181
Lagunitas, CA 94943
(415) 488-4452

Heading cross country for Point Reyes and the Lighthouse from Drakes Beach.

CHAPTER 16

Places of Interest
In and Around
Point Reyes National Seashore

Miwok Indian Village — Morgan Horse Ranch — Point Reyes Lighthouse — Beaches —Tomales Bay State Park —Point Reyes Bird Observatory — Audubon Canyon Ranch — Gulf of the Farallones National Marine Sanctuary

Coast Miwok Indian Village.

KULE LOKLO —A COAST MIWOK CULTURAL EXHIBIT

This replica of a Coast Miwok Indian Village, at Point Reyes National Seashore gives us an idea of the way of life of these Native Americans who lived here for thousands of years before the arrival of Europeans.

The Coast Miwoks lived as hunters and gatherers in Marin and southern Sonoma counties in village communities we call triblets. It is estimated the Coast Miwok Indians inhabited over 100 such villages on the Point Reyes peninsula at the time of Sir Francis Drake's supposed visit in 1579.

Open daily sunrise to sunset. Staffed between 9:30 a.m. and 3:30 p.m. on weekends, at which time additional artifacts may be viewed.

On the first Saturday of every month, you may take part in the ongoing tasks of maintaining the structures and area.

Festivals are offered three times each year. Inquire at the Visitor Center for information regarding dates.

The village was built by volunteers under the direction of the National Park Service and the Miwok Archeological Preserve of Marin.

For additional information, refer to *Kule Loklo and the Coast Miwok Indians*, published by Coastal Parks Association and Miwok Archeological Preserve of Marin(1982), and *The Coast Miwok Indians of the Point Reyes Area*, published by the Point Reyes National Seashore Association(1993). Available for sale at the Visitor Center.

MORGAN HORSE RANCH

A special attraction at Point Reyes National Seashore is the **Morgan Horse Ranch**, located just off the upper parking lot near the Bear Valley Headquarters.

The working horse ranch is one of the locations in the National Park Service where horses are trained for use by Park Rangers. Exhibits, corrals, demonstrations are all part of the ongoing interpretive program of the ranch. Interpretive programs are available to groups by reservation.

Hours: open seven days a week
9 a.m. to 4:30 p.m.
phone: (415) 663-1763

POINT REYES LIGHTHOUSE

The Lighthouse is operated under the auspices of the National Park Service as an Historic Site.

Open 10:00 a.m. to 4:30 p.m. Closed Tuesday and Wednesday.

Over 300 steps lead down the cliff to the Lighthouse. The windswept observation area affords incredible views.

The Lighthouse sits 265 feet above the ocean. Constructed in 1870, it houses the French-built Fresnel lens. The beam is 294 feet above sea level.

March, April and May and November, December and January are the best months for visiting, since there is generally heavy fog during the summer months. Whether you visit for wildflower viewing in May, or whale watching in the winter months, Point Reyes Lighthouse will not disappoint you. The Lighthouse and its environs afford the best vantage point for whale watching at the National Seashore because the point extends so far west into the open sea.

Dress warmly, as it will probably be windy and or foggy. Up to 2700 hours of fog have been recorded yearly.

For more information, call (415) 663-1092 or (415) 699-1534.

BEACHES ACCESSIBLE TO AUTOMOBILES

There are eight beaches in Point Reyes National Seashore which are accessible from the road. For specific road directions, consult your California State Highway map. Five of the beaches — Point Reyes Beach South, Point Reyes Beach North, Abbotts Lagoon and Beach, Kehoe Beach and McClures Beach — are situated on the open sea and are excellent for sunbathing, picknicking and general enjoyment. However, they are all characterized by strong undertow and treacherous rip tides. *Do not go in the water.* Drakes Beach and Limantour Beach are also good for picnicking, sunbathing, sand castling and relaxing. These two beaches, being situated on Drakes Bay, are considered suitable for wading and swimming. Marshall Beach is situated on Tomales Bay where waters are generally calmer, and the beach is more sheltered from the winds. There are no lifeguards anywhere at Drakes or Limantour Beaches, however, and one swims at his or her own risk.

Please remember, it is against the law to remove living organisms from tidepools, except for designated species.

Limantour Beach is perhaps the most popular beach because of its relatively broad beach and dunes. Along with Drakes Beach and Marshall Beach, it is less windy than the other beaches. The access road, which extends some 8.9 miles from the Bear Valley Trailhead to the Limantour parking lot, was severly damaged by the flood of 1982 and is now open.

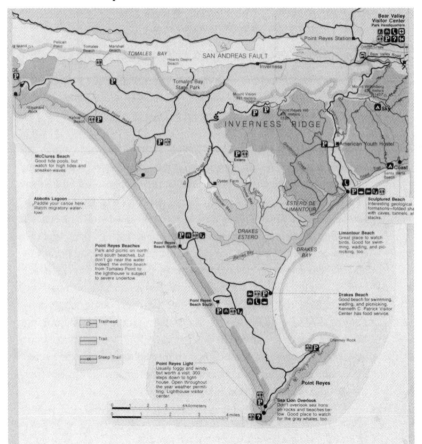

Drakes Beach on Drakes Bay is 15.3 miles from the Bear Valley Trailhead or Olema. You can drive right to the beach, where you will find a spacious parking area, restrooms, picnic tables and a beach house, book store and snackbar. The broad, flat sandy beach is sheltered and excellent for picnicking. Fires are allowed on the beach. There is swimming and, on good days, surfers can be seen riding the breakers. The alleged site of Sir Francis Drake's landing is located 1.5 miles down (southeast) the beach and just inside Drakes Estero. A small plaque commemorates the point where Drake may have careened his *Golden Hind* vessel in June 1579 for repairs. In addition, a granite cross monument to Drake's landing is adjacent to the parking lot. **The Ken Patrick Visitor Center** at Drakes Beach has been expanded to provide additional space for viewing and exhibitry focusing on 16th century exploration and the marine environment. A salt water aquarium has been installed, and is home to plant and animal life from the Bay. A minke whale skeleton is also on display, and you can also experience an eel's eye view of life beyond the surf. Rangers are are on hand to answer your questions. Open weekdays and holidays 10:00 a.m. to 5:00 p.m. Closed for lunch Noon-12:30 p.m. Telephone: (415) 699-1250.

Abbotts Lagoon and Beach is eleven miles by road from the Bear Valley Trailhead or Olema. A small parking area, with restroom facilities, can accommodate some ten to twelve automobiles. An easy 1 1/4 mile walk over level terrain takes you from the parking area to Abbotts Lagoon, some magnificent dunes, and the open sea. Sunbathing and wading are usually best along the mouth of the lagoon. Canoeing is permitted on the Lagoon, which is a migratory bird habitat.

Kehoe Beach, 2.2 miles past the Abbotts Lagoon parking area, is 13.2 miles from the Bear Valley Trailhead. The only parking area is along the shoulder of the road. A 3/4 mile level walk leads to the beach, which offers miles of dunes to choose from in order to picnic or find shelter on windy days. A stile at the road marks the unmaintained trail to the beach. There is a roadside restroom.

McClures Beach is 3.7 miles from Kehoe Beach and 16.9 miles from the Bear Valley Trailhead. A twisty and steep 1/2 mile downhill trail down a ravine takes you to the beach. During storms, or on clear windy days, the breakers put on a dazling display as they smash against the rocks. Exercise caution at high tide when "sneaker waves" sometimes roll in from far out on the sea and come all the way to the base of the cliffs. When the sea is rough, a high tide can roll huge pieces of driftwood onto the beach and up against the cliffs. Beached driftwood offers picnickers protection from wind, and pocket beaches provides shelter for sunbathers. Tidepools abound, making sea urchins, sea anemones, starfish, chitons and hermit crabs fascinating to observe, but remember collecting is prohibited. On calm days and at medium or low tides, McClures Beach is a perfect picnic spot. However, it is advisable to check at the Visitor Center, (415) 663-1092, for weather and tide information before going out to the beach.

Point Reyes Beach North and Point Reyes Beach South are 13.2 miles and 15.9 miles from Bear Valley Trailhead respectively. These two beaches, which are two miles apart, are situated on the open sea along the Great Beach between Kehoe Beach and Point Reyes. One can drive to the beaches' edge at both locations. Restrooms and picnic tables are available at both beaches. The beach is narrow and the surf treacherous along the entire stretch of the Great Beach, so do not swim or even jump breakers at either of these Point Reyes beaches. You will find plenty of dunes, driftwood and space for picnicking. Dogs on leashes and campfires are allowed on the beaches.

Marshall Beach is located on Tomales Bay and involves a 1 1/2 mile walk, including a steep trail, from the parking area to the beach. Drive from the Bear Valley Trailhead past Inverness on Sir Francis Drake Blvd. 7.5 miles to the junction and follow Pierce Point Road about 1.7 miles to the entrance to Tomales Bay State Park. Just past the State Park entrance there is a dirt road coming in from the right. This road, the Marshall Beach road, climbs abruptly through a conifer forest for 150 yards or more, and levels off in open country. 2.6 miles from Sir Francis Drake Blvd. you will come to the Marshall Beach parking area, which is marked with a sign. Along the Marshall Beach road you will observe some junctions with other ranch roads. Stay left and follow the Park Service signs directing you to the parking area. From the parking area it is 1.6 miles on an old ranch road to the beach.

The sandy beach is secluded, and usually less inhabited than the other beaches of Point Reyes National Seashore. Tomales Bay does not generally have a heavy surf or undertow and is, therefore, better for wading and swimming. However, Tomales Bay sometimes has sharks and there is no lifeguard on duty. Restroom facilities are available.

TOMALES BAY STATE PARK

8:00 a.m. to 8:00 p.m. daily during summer.

8:00 a.m. to sunset during the rest of the year.

Western shore of Tomales Bay. 3 miles north of Inverness, off Pierce Point Road.

(415) 699-1140.

The park features Coast Miwok Indian relics, Bishop pines, sandy beaches, many different species of plants, animals and birds. Park beaches are Shell, Pebble, Heart's Desire and Indian. There is fishing from shore, picnic tables and swimming. The water is around 68 to 70 degrees during the summer. A paved road leads to Heart's Desire Beach. Heart's Desire is considered one of the best family picnic beaches in the area.

Tomales Bay State Park is a preserve for the Bishop Pine. A memorial grove of the pines is dedicated to pioneer botanist Willis Linn Jepson.

POINT REYES BIRD OBSERVATORY

Mesa Road 4.5 miles north of Bolinas. 1/2 mile south of Palomarin Trailhead.

Open daily, April through summer. Otherwise open Wednesdays and weekends.

The Observatory is the only full time ornithological research station in the United States.

Birdbanding takes place early in the morning from April 1 through Thanksgiving.

Lookout Museum.   Special tours can be arranged by calling (415) 868-1221.

AUDUBON CANYON RANCH

Audubon Canyon Ranch is a wildlife sanctuary and center for nature education. It is located on Shoreline Highway approximately 13 miles south of Point Reyes Station.

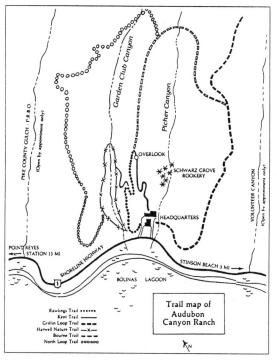

Rawlings Trail ••••••
Kent Trail ————
Griffin Loop Trail — — —
Harwell Nature Trail —x—
Bourne Trail — — —
North Loop Trail ooooooo

Trail map of
Audubon
Canyon Ranch

The Ranch is open March 1 through July 4. The public is welcome on Saturdays, Sundays and holidays 10 a.m. to 4 p.m. For appointments, or more information, call (415) 383-1644 or write: Audubon Canyon Ranch, 4900 Shoreline Highway, Stinson Beach, CA 94970.

No charge is made for visits, but contributions are welcome. They are needed for the maintenance and development of the Ranch and Nature Center and are tax deductible.

Audubon Canyon Ranch contains a major heronry of Great Blue Herons and Great Egrets. Each year these birds nest in the tops of the tall redwood trees. They find fish and crustaceans for themselves and for their young in the water and tidelands of nearby Bolinas Lagoon.

A steep 1/2 mile trail leads to Henderson Overlook. From the platform, at which telescopes are provided, you will enjoy a rare view into the nests of the Great Blue Heron and Great Egrets. A naturalist is at the Overlook to interpret the dynamics of the breeding colony and assist with the telescopes.

In 1969 the Ranch was designated a Registered National Natural Landmark by the Department of the Interior and the National Park Service for its exceptional value in illustrating the natural history of the United States.

GULF OF THE FARALLONES
NATIONAL MARINE SANCTUARY

The **Gulf of the Farallones National Marine Sanctuary** covers waters adjacent to the coast north and south of the Point Reyes Headlands between Bodega Head and Rocky Point and the Farallon Islands, including Noonday Rock. It encompasses approximately 948 square nautical miles. The shoreward boundary follows the mean high tide line and seaward limit of Point Reyes National Seashore. Between Bodega Head and the Point Reyes Headlands, it extends 3 nautical miles beyond state waters and includes the waters within 12 nautical miles of the Farallon Islands, and between the Islands and the mainland from the Headlands to Rocky Point.

The Sanctuary was designated to protect an important part of our nation's marine resources.

The National Oceanic and Atmospheric Administration manages the Sanctuary through the Sanctuary Programs Office of its Office of Coastal Zone Management. The program emphasizes the protection of special marine areas for the long-term benefit and enjoyment of the public. Research and educational programs have been initiated to improve our understanding and appreciation of the site's resources, and promote their wise use.

For additional information, contact:

Gulf of the Farallones National Marine Sanctuary
National Oceanic & Atmospheric Administration
GGNRA, Fort Mason
San Francisco, CA 94123
telephone: (415) 556-3509

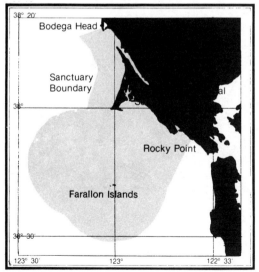

Gulf of the Farallones National Marine Sanctuary

Whale watching at Point Reyes near the lighthouse.

CHAPTER 17

Whale Watching

*Vantage Points — Eschrichtius Robustus —
Terminology — Appearance — Habits —*

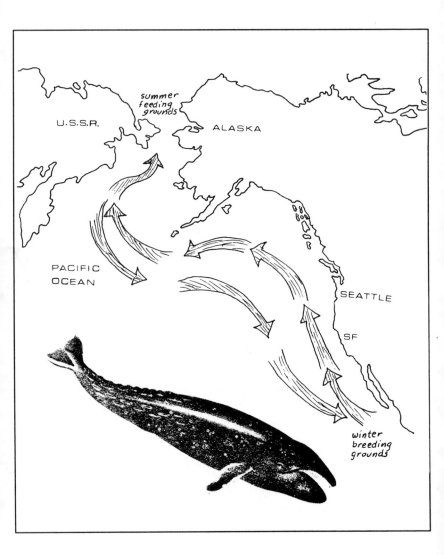

summer
feeding
grounds

U.S.S.R.

ALASKA

PACIFIC
OCEAN

SEATTLE

SF

winter
breeding
grounds

During their southern migration along the western coast of North America, whales seek waters much closer to the shore than they would otherwise. This effort, by the calving mothers, to avoid the high seas, makes them extraordinarily visible. The migration begins in mid to late December, and is usually at its heaviest in January. In February there are fewer whales, and by March one sees only a few stragglers. Since whales swim at a speed of three to five miles an hour, their progress is easily charted.

When watching for whales at Point Reyes National Seashore one must consider the best vantage points, and when one is most likely to see whales.

VANTAGE POINTS

- Point Reyes itself. The most commanding view is near the Point Reyes Lighthouse.

- On the Coast Trail some 300-600 vertical feet above Miller Point. An excellent view of Drakes Bay.

- On the Woodward Valley Trail, at the point where the trail breaks out into the open at 500' above sea level. Face the ocean, then look 45 degrees to your right to a small nearby hill some 50 vertical feet higher than where you are standing. Walk 100 yards to the top of this hill.

- Along the Coast Trail near Wildcat Beach, there is a spot amid pine trees, near some old boarded up forts. Just past the pine trees, there is a dramatic view of Drakes Bay.

- Along the Coast Trail, in the first two miles north of

Palomarin Trailhead, there are places with a good view of the ocean.

• Along the Coast Trail from where it crosses Coast Creek and where it turns inland towards the Hostel there are a number of locations just west of the trail where one can have a good view of Drakes Bay.   Above Kelham Beach, at the promontory of Point Resistance, above Secret Beach, and above Sculptured Beach.

A good pair of binoculars is recommended for anyone searching for whales at Point Reyes National Seashore.

Dress warmly, as it will probably be windy and/or foggy at the Lighthouse. The Lighthouse area is really very windy, and on such days the wind can't be half as strong elsewhere in the Seashore. You would do well to call the Lighthouse Visitor Center in advance for a weather and whale activity report, (415) 669-1534.

The Oceanic Society Expeditions offer naturalist-guided whale-watching out of San Francisco and Half Moon Bay. Also Three Baja Expeditions can bring you close up and sometimes within touching distance of Grays. Call Whale Watch (415) 474-3385.

ESCHRICTHIUS ROBUSTUS

This is the best known of the great whales in California, and the one most often seen. Gray whales feed in the summer, in the western Bering Sea and Arctic Ocean in the winter.

The grays migrate down the Pacific Coast from Alaska to Baja.

There, in various of the bays and lagoons of Baja California and the mainland (most notably thr Scammon Lagoon) the females have their calves and breed. Gestation is 13 months. Later, in March and April, they reverse the route, plying their way back up along the coast— only this time not quite as close to the land.

They travel to Baja fairly close to the shore, often coming within a few hundred yards of some points, or even into the surf zone.

The grays travel around 13,000 miles on their round trip, and the trip takes 2 1/2 months. The distance is calculated to be 60 to 80 nautical miles per day, at a speed of 4 knots for a 15 to 10 hour day. They frequently raise their heads out of water to look around and get their bearings. Whales are believed to find their way on the long migration by memory and vision.

TERMINOLOGY

Spouting. The visual release of vapor from the air held in the lungs under great pressure and therefore cooled. The vapor has quite a smell. Also called blowing.

Pod. A group of whales, all the way fro, 3 or 4 to 20 or 30, traveling together.

Breaching. To leap out of the water.

Baleen Whales. One of two groups of whales, the other g:oup is toothed. These whales have no teeth. Instead, they have sheets of a fringed horny material, hanging from their upper jaws. They use this to strain out plankton. It is interesting that the largest of all

Dead whale at beach below Arch Rock Overlook.

animals feed low on the food chain, at a level where food is most abundant.

APPEARANCE

Gray whales reach 35 to 50 feet in length and around 20 to 40 tons in weight. The calf is 15 to 16 feet long at birth. Females produce one calf every two years, at the most.

The whale is black, mottled with gray, and covered with barnacles and whitish scars. There is no dorsal fin, but there is a small, distinct ridge on the back, at about the location where a fin would be, followed by a series of bumps.

A thick layer of fat or blubber helps the whales combat the cold ocean water.

Whales have almost lost their hair, but not quite. A gray whale has over 100 hairs on its chin and the tip of its upper jaw.

HABITS

The gray whale, one of the baleen whales, feeds mainly on small crustaceans, though to some extent on small fish as well. Feeding takes place largely, it is believed, during the four months of the year spent in the north. There is some evidence of feeding during the eight months spent in migration and in the lagoons.

Sleep is accompolished by taking short naps, while the whale drifts motionless near the surface. The gray whale, sleeping in the lagoons, breathes every 5 to 10 minutes.

Whales have a sophisticated method of communication consisting of clicks, hums, whines, whistles, etc. This is often called "singing."

The whale is hunted for its oil, its bone and for food. The toll on the whales has been so heavy that it has threatened their continued existence. In 1938 an international agreement giving the gray whales complete protection, and regulating the taking of whales, was put into effect. The gray whale is an excellent example of how a formerly endangered species can flourish under complete protection. However, the fate of many whale species is precarious.

More information about whales and whale migration is available from the following organizations in California:

General Whale, Alameda	(415)865-5550
Project Jonah, San Francisco	(415)205-9846
Greenpeace, San Francisco	(415)474-6767
Oceanic Society, San Francisco	(415)441-1104
Lawrence Hall of Science, Berkeley	(415)642-5132
The American Cetacean Society, San Pedro	(213)548-6279

Point Resistance in the foreground and Double Point from Woodward Valley Trail.

CHAPTER 18

DIRECTORY

General Services — Emergency —

Service Stations — Campgrounds —

Where to Stay — Where to Eat —

General Stores

The Coast Trail between Palomarin and the Lake Ranch.

GENERAL SERVICES

INFORMATION CENTERS

Bear Valley Visitor Center	(415) 663-1092
Bear Valley Weather, Whale, & Info	(415) 663-9029
Ken Patrick Visitor Center	(415) 669-1250
Lighthouse Visitor Center	(415) 669-1534
Morgan Horse Ranch	(415) 663-1763
Tomales Bay State Park	(415) 6691140

STABLES

Five Brooks Stables	(415) 663-1570
The Inn at Point Reyes Ranch	(415) 663-8888
Stewart's Horse Camp	(415) 663-1362

OYSTER COMPANIES

Johnson's Oyster Farm	(415) 669-1149
Tomales Bay Oyster Co.	(415) 663-1242
Hog Island Oyster Comapany	(415 663-9218

BIKE RENTALS

Trailhead Rentals	(415) 663-1958

COIN LAUNDRY

Olema Ranch Campground	(415) 663-1041

POST OFFICES

Olema	(415) 663-1761
Point Reyes Station	(415) 663-1305
Inverness	(415) 669-1675

WHALE WATCHING BOAT TRIPS

Oceanic Society Expeditions   (415) 474-3385

EDUCATION CENTERS

Point Reyes Field Seminars   (415) 663-1200
Point Reyes Bird Observatory   (415) 868-1221
Marine Mammal Center   (415) 331-7325
Marin Wildlife Center   (415) 454-6961

Tune 1610 AM—As you drive out to the Lighthouse tune your car radio to 1610 AM to hear updated Park Information. You will hear of weather and traffic conditions, special events, and natural history notes. As you drive along Bear Valley Road to the park Headquarters area in Olema, tune in for information on the Bear Valley area including naturalist activities.

TELEPHONE DEVICE FOR THE DEAF

Bear Valley Visitor Center   (415) 663-1092

EMERGENCY

ALL EMERGENCIES CALL   **911**

MEDICAL SERVICES

West Marin Medical Center   (415) 663-1082
Point Reyes Clinic   (415) 663-8666

SERVICE STATIONS

INVERNESS

Drake Highway Garage   (415) 669-1017

POINT REYES STATION

Bud's Auto Service   (415) 663-1177
Cheda's Chevrolet   (415) 663-1227

OLEMA

Olema Ranch Campground (gas only)   (415) 663-8001

CAMPGROUNDS

Point Reyes National Seashore (walk-in) (415) 663-1092
Olema Ranch Campground   (415) 663-8001
Samuel P. Taylor State Park   (415) 488-9897
Golden Gate National Recreation Area (walk-in)
                                         (415) 331-1540
Mount Tampalpais State Park (walk-in)   (415) 388-2070
Lawsons Landing (Dillon Beach   (707) 878-2443

WHERE TO STAY

Bed & Breakfast Cottages of Point Reyes	(415) 663-9445
Coastal Lodging of West Marin	(415) 663-1351
Inns of Points Reyes	(415) 663-1420
Point Reyes Youth Hostal	(415) 663-8811
Seashore Bed & Breakfasts	(415) 663-9373
West Marin Chamber of Commerce	(415) 663-9232
West Marin Network	(415) 663-9543

WHERE TO EAT

OLEMA

Olema Farmhouse	(415) 663-1264
Olema Inn	(415) 663-9559

POINT REYES

Station House Cafe	(415) 663-1515
Mike's Cafe	(415) 663-1536
Taqueria La Quinta	(415) 663 8868

INVERNESS

Barnaby's	(415) 669-1041
Gray Whale	(415) 669-1244
Manka's Czech Restaurant	(415) 669-1034
Perry's Deli	(415) 663-1491
Vladimir's Czech Restaurant	(415) 669-1021
Knave of Hearts Bakery	(415) 663-1236
Inverness Inn	(415) 669-1109

DRAKES BEACH

Drakes Beach Cafe	(415) 663-1297

MARSHALL

Nick's Cove	(415) 6631033
Tony's Seafood	(415) 663-1107

GENERAL STORES

INVERNESS

Inverness Store	(415) 669-1041
Inverness Park Groceries	(415) 663-1491

POINT REYES STATION

Whale of a Deli	(415) 663-1495
Palace Market	(415) 663-1016

OLEMA

Olema Store	(415) 663-1479

BAKERIES

Bolinas Bay Bakery	(415) 868-0211
Gray Whale Bakery	(415) 669-1244
Knave of Hearts Bakery	(415) 663-1236

Limantour Estero marsh lands.

APPENDIX

Bear Valley Visitor Center

Climate

Landscape & Cover Type

Birdwatching

Native & Exotic Deer

Fishing & Marine Life

Harbor Seals

The following articles by Point Reyes National Park Service rangers have been reprinted with permission. Exceptionally well done, we feel they make an important addition and contribution to our guide. We would like to express our appreciation to the National Park Service personnel at Point Reyes for allowing their inclusion.

Bear Valley Trail at Divide Meadow.

BEAR VALLEY VISITOR CENTER

From a distance, the Bear Valley Visitor Center blends into the surrounding meadows and forest with the overall effect of a large old barn. The Center houses a library, collection room, auditorium, offices, and 2,500 square feet of exhibits about Point Reyes.

This Visitor Center was constructed in 1983 utilizing funds from two major private foundations: the William Field Charitable Fund and the San Francisco Foundation (Buck Fund). Each foundation donated $700,000 to cover the total $1.4 million cost of the building. This 7,600 square foot structure was designed by Henrik Bull, of the San Francisco firm of Bull, Stockwell, and Volkmann. The interior exhibits were designed by Dan Quan, of San Francisco. Fabrication of the exhibits was completed by Greyhound Exhibit Group, also from San Francisco.

The exhibits are divided into several sections: 1) physical aspects of Point Reyes, including a weather station which indicates wind velocity and direction, temperature, and rainfall, and a seismograph; 2) history of the Miwoks, early explorers, ranching, shipwrecks, and the Park itself; 3) plant and animal communities of Point Reyes.

The interior exhibits (dioramas) were constructed by Fred Funk Exhibits, who used many interesting techniques. To preserve the flora two methods were utilized. The two large trees were actually "pickled." They were first cut down and divided into small sections, then the sections were submerged in a glycerin bath for a pickling effect. Finally, each tree was reconstructed to its original form. The other method utilized for constructing plants was "vacuum forming." Leaves were fabricated from molds and formed out of plastic. Many of the animals in the exhibit are from roadway accidents, and using taxidermy techniques, preserved for the exhibits. Many visitors are intrigued with the "water" in some of the exhibits. The water is actually a casting resin that was poured over a dark soil background.

Below is a list of birds and animals that you will find in the exhibits.

BIRDS

Osprey (and nest)
California Quail
Raven
Red-tailed Hawk
Brown Pelican
Dark-eyed Junco
Northern Harrier
Acorn Woodpecker
California Towhee
Northern Saw-whet Owl
Red-shouldered Hawk
Northern Pintail
Long-billed Dowitcher
Great-Horned Owl
Common Egret
Western Gull
Western Sandpiper
Pelagic Cormorant
California Gull

Dunlin
Northern Flicker
Heerman's Gull
Marbled Godwit
Brown Creeper
Bufflehead
American Wigeon
Red-winged Blackbird
Surf Scoter
Mallard
Stellar's Jay
Snowy Egret
Great Blue Heron
Marsh Wren
Common Murre
Brandt's Cormorant
Black-bellied Plover
Turkey Vulture
Tufted Puffin

ANIMALS

Muskrat
Gopher Snake
Grey Squirrel
Brushrabbit
Deer Mouse
Pond Turtle
Black-tailed Deer
Striped Skunk
Woodrat
Bobcat
Sonoma Chipmunk
Mussel

Gopher
Jack Rabbit
Anemone
Raccoon
Gray Whale Skull
Black Chiton
Harbor Seal, Female
Harbor Seal, Pup
Badger
Sea Star
Long-tailed Weasel
Barnacle
Gray Fox

CLIMATE

Point Reyes Peninsula's climate is characterized by warm, dry summers and cool, rainy winters, similar to the type of climate that prevails on the Mediterranean. The United States Coast Guard Station, located at the extreme western tip of the peninsula, has kept weather records for at least 80 years. There is also a weather observation station at the Bear Valley Headquarters area of the National Seashore.

There are constant winds of moderate to strong velocity on the exposed headlands and outer beaches. During most of the year, particularly in the summer, prevailing wind direction is northwesterly. There is a tendency for the winds to shift to the south during the winter. The greatest wind velocities occur in November and December during infrequent southerly gales. *Winds have been clocked up to 130 miles per hour* at the Coast Guard Station on the Point, but the annual maximum wind velocity is 43 miles per hour. Winds are much lighter on the eastern side of the Inverness

Ridge, but it is an unusual day that does not bring some afternoon breezes to Point Reyes.

Headlands and beaches on the Pacific Coast are subjected to frequent heavy fogs. During most of the year, the water temperatures near the coast are lower than that of the ocean further to the west. The cooling effect of these frigid coastal waters on the warmer moist air moving past produces fog, which blankets the ocean for more than 50 miles or more off the shore and often smothers the beaches with heavy fog, reminiscent of the "thicke mists and stynkinge fogges" Sir Francis Drake's men complained of when he visited the northern California coast in June, 1579. Such heavy fogs are most common in the months of July, August and September.

Sunshine and higher temperatures occur inland. The east side of Inverness Ridge and the beaches of Tomales Bay are sheltered from the summit of the ridge westward to the ocean, leaving sunny areas for picnicing and swimming. *Inland temperatures in the summer are often 20 degrees warmer than temperatures on the Headlands and outer coast.*

Rainfall averages about 11.5 inches per year out on the Point where the Lighthouse is located, with the heaviest rainfall coming in December, January, February and March. A few miles inland the rainfall is much greater, averaging about 36 inches a year at Bear Valley Headquarters of the National Seashore. Although there is scarcely any rain from mid-April to October, the night and morning coastal fogs condensing on the trees keep the wooded hills moistened. The moderating influence of the Pacific Ocean creates an even climate with no great extremes of heat or cold. The average monthly temperatures differ only about 28 degrees from high to low throughout the entire year.

LANDSCAPE & COVER TYPE

The flora of Point Reyes National Seashore shows that the peninsula has long been the meeting ground of northern and southern California Coast Range floras. A forest of Douglas fir grows on the eastern slopes of Inverness Ridge and in some of the deeper canyons facing the ocean. Bishop pines, unique to the California coast, occur on the northern half on the Inverness Ridge. A small grove of coast redwoods in the southern part of the Seashore adds to the ecological variety. Mingled with the Douglas firs, or flanking them at lower levels, are groves of broadleaf trees consisting of madrone, California bay, tanbark oak, live oak, maple and red alder. A profusion of shrubs includes rhododendron, ceanothus (wild lilac), honeysuckle, wild rose, wax myrtle and black huckleberry. Woodland is interspersed with grassland in which the California buckeye is a common and conspicuous feature. The ranges of five species of plants are confined exclusively to the Point Reyes peninsula. Two endemic manzanitas grow only on Mount Tamalpais and the peninsula.

On the seaward side of the ridge the brush covered slopes of the hills include thickets of chaparral-type growth. Wind-swept coastal bush lupines, kinnikinnick, gumweed, sea thrift, coyote brush, and succulent plants live on the maritime bluffs. The small valleys in the brushlands contain islands of coast live oak and wind-pruned California bay. Some twenty-five species of shrubs grow on the sides of these brushy hills. Coyote brush is a common colonizer and may occur as an almost pure stand. Poison oak is omnipresent in both brushland and woodland. A versatile plant, poison oak may occur as a clump or thicket three or more feet high, or as a vine climbing up tree trunks, or as a ground runner.

The rolling lowlands facing the sea are covered with extensive grasslands. A profusion of wildflowers decorates the area in springtime. Much of the grassland may be due largely to agricultural practices. Over the years the land has been plowed, planted to crops, and then seeded to non-native grasses for pasture. Stock grazing for more than a century has drastically altered the native grassland complex. In the pastoral zone grow many exotics; Monterey cypress and blue gum eucalyptus are fairly common in the Seashore.

Along the dunes and beaches the dramatic see-saw struggle of plants to bind the shifting sands and establish themselves in spite of wind and waves is a fascinating ecological story. Many of the dune plants, particulary the lupines, produce a notable wildflower spectacle. Since the introduction of European dune grass and ice plant, the flora and topography of the sand dunes has changed dramatically. Some plants unique to the dunes of Point Reyes must be carefully monitored to insure their protection.

The fresh water marshes, although of limited extent, are of great interest to plant ecologists. The swales lying behind sand dunes which have dammed natural drainages produce a distinctive group of spring plants. The salt water marshes, with growths of pickleweed and sea-blite, are vital feeding grounds for a great variety of waterfowl. As a result of the diversified plant life and climate, the wildlife of the peninsula shows a corresponding diversity, ranging from salt water shore birds to the birds and mammals typical of dense mountain forests.

BIRDWATCHING

Point Reyes National Seashore offers some of the finest birdwatching in the United States. More than 70,000 acres of habitat harbor an incredible variety of bird life. Over 400 avian species have been observed in the park and on adjacent waters.

The park's coastal location and its wealth of unspoiled habitats—estuaries, grasslands, coastal scrub and forest—all attract many migrating and wintering birds. The projection of the peninsula some 10 miles seaward from the geologic "mainland" make Point Reyes National Seashore a landing spot for many vagrants—birds that have made errors in navigation and thus are unexpected in this area.

All these factors account for the Point Reyes area consistently reporting one of the highest tallies in the nation every year during the Christmas bird count.

Five Brooks Pond. In winter, green-backed heron, hooded merganser, ring-necked duck, and grebes can be seen. In grasses and trees watch for pileated woodpecker, swallows, accipiters, warblers, and thrushes.

Bear Valley. A great variety of land birds frequent the numerous habitats along the trails over Inverness Ridge to the ocean— warblers, sparrows, kinglets, thrushes, wrens, woodpeckers, hummingbirds, crossbills, and owls.

Olema Marsh. The largest fresh water marsh in Marin County supports marsh, water and riparian species including belted kingfishers. At high tide, egrets and herons feed on rails and voles.

Tomales Bay and Bolinas Lagoon.   Important for wintering waterfowl including three species of scoters and Brant geese; osprey, shore birds, herons and egrets all year.

Tomales Point.   Outstanding for finding birds of prey during fall and winter months. In winter look for owls, peregrine falcons, and hawks. Passerines feed on seeds and insects in this area.

Abbotts Lagoon.   Excellent for winter ducks and raptors. Black-shouldered kites are commonly seen in winter and fall. This is also a sensitive nesting area for the endangered snowy plover. Please tread carefully on the sandy beaches during the spring and early summer months.

Estero Trail.   An old pine plantation provides winter roosting habitat for long-eared and great-horned owls. Look for water and shore birds such as great egrets, great blue herons and loons in the Estero. Watch for hawks above the grasslands.

Drakes and Limantour Estero.   Abundant water, shore and marsh birds including grebes, herons, egrets, terns and loons.

Outer Peninsula Grasslands.   Look for winter vagrant ground dwellers including plovers and longspurs and migrating and resident hawks. Watch along the roadside for flocks of perching birds.

Ranchlands.   Dairy ranches are Seashore property leased back to the ranchers. *Please respect property rights and privacy.* Avoid buildings, gardens and farmyards. Leave all gates just as you find them and do not block any gates with cars. Consider carpooling to these areas in order to reduce traffic congestion. In spring and particularly fall, see unusual vagrant passerines and raptors.

Lighthouse rocks and cliff areas. Brown pelicans in fall, numerous pelagic and migrating species in spring. Most common spring pelagics include cormorants, common murres, pigeon guillemots, loons, and scoters. Keep your eyes out for black oystercatchers all year. Peregrine falcons are occasionally spotted. Tufted puffins are occasionally seen in the spring and early summer.

NATIVE & EXOTIC DEER

When traveling through Point Reyes National Seashore deer are a common sight. The Seashore has three wild and reproducing species of deer living within its boundaries. Occasionally they intermingle when feeding, but they do not interbreed.

The native black-tailed deer (Odocoileus hemiounus columbianus) are distributed throughout the 100 square miles of the Seashore. They can be seen any time of the day, but evening brings many deer out to feed in open pastures where they are more visible.

black-tailed deer

Although they are often seen in large temporary feeding groups, black-tailed deer do not form herds. Unlike other deer, the black-tailed do not migrate and may spend their entire life within the same area.

In October the bucks enter rut, or mating season, and gather the females into harems for breeding. Fawns are born in April and May, and are covered with white spots for the first three and a half months. Does will establish a territory to protect their fawns from other females. If startled, a fawn will lie down in the brush while the doe attempts to draw off a predator. The absence of scent further protects a growing fawn.

Every year the bucks shed their antlers around January and begin to grow new ones the following spring. The covering of velvet which provides the antlers with food and oxygen is rubbed off in early fall. Despite popular belief, the number of points on a set of antlers does not indicate the age of the buck.

axis deer

The exotic axis deer (Axis axis), or chital, are native to India and Ceylon. Introduced by Dr. Millard Ottinger, a San Francisco surgeon, who also operated a ranch on the west side of Mount Vision, eight were brought in from the San Francisco Zoo in 1947 and 1948. Today their numbers are estimated to be between four and five hundred. The axis deer range from McClures Beach in the north, to Limantour Estero in the south.

Axis deer are the most sociable of all deer and may be seen in herds as large as 75 to 100. Their native name of chital refers to the white spots which are visible all year against their reddish-brown coat. They are further distinguished by the dark stripe running the length of their back, and the white "bib" present. The bucks carry long antlers that are forked at the top, with another fork near the base. Antlers are shed in the winter.

Fawns of all sizes are seen throughout the year, indicating that impregnation and birth occur during all seasons. The axis deer feed and hide in the coastal scrub, but are often grazing in open grassland. When alarmed, a loud, sharp "yowp" is given that alerts the herd. If danger is close, the herd takes off usually led by a mature doe.

Fallow deer (Dama Dama) are native to the Mediterranean region of Europe and Asia Minor. In England, noblemen traditionally kept semi-domesticated fallow deer in their deer parks, where centuries of selective breeding produced numerous coat colorations. Colors range from white to buff to charcoal with lighter underparts, and brown with white spots. Fallow deer in America stem from the English stock. The color type of an individual deer does not change through its lifetime.

fallow deer

Fallow bucks have large, palmate antlers much like those of moose. The older bucks tend to herd separately from the does, except during the rut in October. Their antlers are not shed until April and the velvet of the new antlers is shed in August. Fawns are born in mid-June, rarely occurring as twins. A fawn is often a different color type from its mother.

Between 1942 and 1954, 28 fallow deer were purchased from the

San Francisco Zoo by Dr. Millard Ottinger. Today their population is estimated at about 500. They have spread as far south as Double Point, and as far north as Tomales Bay State Park.

Recent studies on the exotic deer indicate that their population numbers are increasing. Unchecked populations result in competition for forage with native black-tailed deer. Due to this potential problem, the National Park Service has initiated a program of exotic deer management. This management program consists of continued research to determine the optimum population levels, and deer reduction to keep the population within these limits. The selective deer reduction is performed by Park personnel.

FISHING & MARINE LIFE INFORMATION

REGULATIONS. People 16 years of age and older must have in their possession a valid California fishing license for the taking of any kind of fish, mollusk, invertebrate, amphibian, crustacean or reptile (except for rattlesnakes). No amphibians or reptiles may be taken. *All* those who are fishing are responsible for adhering to all *fishing hours, limits, methods and other fishing regulations* found in the pamphlet "California Sport Fishing Regulations", obtainable at stores selling fishing licenses, bait and equipment. Regulations are strictly enforced. CAUTION: Regulations may be very specific to certain areas. You must refer to the sport fishing pamphlet to obtain that information.

RESTRICTED AREAS. Point Reyes Headlands Reserve and **Estero De Limantour Reserve** are set aside as **reserves** and *all* marine life is protected within their boundaries. In the **Duxbury Reef Reserve**, *some* invertebrates and fish can be taken.

Fishing in all creeks and streams within the Seashore is prohibited.

Refer to fishing regulations for specific information. Maps showing boundaries of reserves and fishing areas are available at visitor centers.

There are no public fishing piers within the Seashore.

SALTWATER FISH. See "California Sport Fishing Regulations" for specific regulations.

Drakes Bay — flounder, sea trout, perch, leopard shark and rockfish.

Tomales Bay — flounder, halibut, jack smelt, lingcod, redtail perch, salmon, striped bass, sturgeon and trout.

North and South Beaches — serf perch, flounder, sea trout. Beware of extremely heavy surf.

Sharks — angel, sevengil, sand, leopard and great white sharks have been taken in Drakes and Tomales Bay. No season, no limit, all sizes.

Poke Pole Fishing — done in tide pools along Palomarin Beach, McClures Beach, and other rocky shores for blenny eels and rockfish.

FRESH WATER FISH. See "California Sport Fishing Regulations" for specific regulations.

Trout, Bass, Bluegil, Crappie — Many reservoirs and lakes in the Seashore were stocked in the past when under private ownership. While the National Park Service has not restocked them, fishing remains fair in some of the lakes. Fishing is allowed in some creeks and streams within the Seashore.

Nearby Fishing Areas — Nicasio Reservoir, Lagunitas Creek (Papermill Creek) below the Highway 1 bridge (closed Oct. 1 - Dec. 31), Walker Creek below the Highway 1 bridge.

FISHING ACCESS. Access to many areas within the Seashore is limited. Many areas can be reached only by foot trails, and some beaches only by boat. Parts of the northern grasslands are still operating ranches. Please respect the rights of these ranchers when crossing pasture lands.

SALTWATER INVERTEBRATES. See "California Sport Fishing Regulations" for specific regulations.

Invertebrates may not be taken from any tidepool or from any other area between high tide mark and 1,000 feet beyond low tide mark in Point Reyes National Seashore, except for: abalone, chiones, clams, cockles, crabs, lobsters, rock scallops, sea urchins, native oysters and ghost shrimp. Mussels may be taken in all areas except in State Park System Reserves or Natural Preserves.

QUARANTINE. From May 1 through October 31, the California State Department of Health places annual quarantine on mussels and occasionally Washington clams. During this period, mussels and the dark part of all clams and scallops may concentrate a toxic material that is highly poisonous to humans. Only the white meat of clams and scallops should be prepared for human consumption. Check with the park visitor centers if you have any questions.

Clams — one-half hour before sunrise to one-half hour after sunset.

Gaper or horseneck —Tomales Bay and Drakes Estero. Limit: 10.

Washington —Tomales Bay and Drakes Estero. Limit: 10.

Geoduck — mouth of Tomales Bay. Limit: 3.

All gaper, Washington and geoduck clams dug, regardless of size or broken condition, must be retained until bag limit is reached. *Please refill holes after digging to reduce damage to environment.*

Cockles — Tomales Bay and Drakes Estero. Minimum size: 1 1/2 inches in greatest diameter. Limit: 50.

Mussels — McClures and Kehoe Beach. Limit: 10 pounds.

Oysters — cultivated and sold commercially in Drakes Bay and Tomales Bay.

Abalone — Palomarin Beach, McClures Beach, Tomales Point. Minimum size: Red abalone, 7 inches; Black abalone, 5 inches. Limit 4. All legal size abalones detached must be retained and detaching shall stop when bag limit is reached. Season: April-June, Aug.-Nov. Hours: 1/2 hour before sunrise to 1/2 hour after sunset only.

Crabs — Tomales Bay. Red rock crabs, minimum size: 4 inches. Limit:35. Season: all year. Dungeness crabs, minimum size: 6 1/4 inches. Limit: 10. Season: 2nd Tuesday in November through June 30.

HARBOR SEALS

Harbor seals (Phoca Vitulina) are distinguished from other species of seals and from sea lions by their dark and light spotted coats and their lack of external ear flaps. Their average length when grown is about five feet, and males and females are nearly identical. They can be found along the Pacific Coast from the Bering Sea to Baja California, sometimes hauled out on the Seashore in large numbers. Because they are non-migratory, they may be seen year round.

Seals and sea lions haul out because they cannot maintain their body temperature if they stay in the cold water all the time. On land, they can absorb the heat from the sun. Their preferred hauling grounds are sandy beaches, mud flats, and reefs. Many of the beaches and mud flats along Point Reyes National Seashore are popular hauling out spots for the harbor seals. Pupping season here occurs from March into May, during which time the number of seals present at any given time at the hauling sites reaches a peak.

While hiking along the wild wet shores of the Pacific in the spring, you may come across a seal pup alone on the beach. Don't assume that it has been abandoned. If you see a lone pup, inform the Park Service of your observation, but do not touch or move the pup. The mother is probably in the water nearby feeding. It is very difficult to reunite a mother and pup after the pup has been moved, and practically impossible to raise a pup in captivity.

A harbor seal pup can swim at birth but pups are almost always born on land. Pups are born with thick fur that insulates them from the cold until they put on weight. Although mother seals are extremely attentive, they will frequently leave a newborn pup on the beach while they seek food. When she returns from feeding, the mother will groom, caress and nuzzle her baby pup constantly, as well as nurse it with her extremely rich milk. The rich milk (about 48% fat) helps the pup to put on weight rapidly. When the pup can swim faster the mother will keep it close by her until the time of weaning, at around two months.

Habor seals are extremely sensitive to disturbance. They may leave their hauling areas temporarily—or even permanently—after harassment by people, boats or aircraft, or other equipment. Historically they have abandoned hauling sites altogether due to a high incidence of human disturbance, as was the case in San Francisco Bay. To help preserve this sensitive and unique creature, people should take care not to make their presence known either visually or audibly when they come across an individual or group of harbor seals, as the seals may flee into the water immediately when they sight a human.

The Marine Mammal Protection Act of 1972 includes harbor seals, along with sea lions, whales, porpoises, sea otters, and other mammals, under federal protection. This law prohibits killing or harassing these shy creatures in any manner. Any human action that causes a change in the behavior of a marine mammal is considered harassment.

What is the Point Reyes experience?

… a meal at one of the excellent local places after a day of hiking… a bed & breakfast stay …

... picnicking, biking, riding ...

… shopping at the local boutiques and stores…

...learning about the park from rangers at the Visitor Center...

*…whale watching
at the lighthouse…*

…crashing waves,
wildflowers,
waterfalls,
meadows,
open trails …

On different visits it is different things,

different moods, vistas, climate… but always very special.

Native Californian Phil Arnot is an active and highly regarded mountaineer and explorer. He has hiked extensively in the Olympic Mountains of Washington, the Cascade Mountains of Oregon and Washington, New Zealand, South America, and the High Sierras of Yosemite and Sequoia National Parks.

He has made numerous ascents, including Mt. McKinley and hiked over 8000 trail and off-trail miles in the western wilderness.

He leads wilderness trips throughout the Western United States, Alaska and Point Reyes National Seashore.

Arnot has co-authored the books *Run for Your Life* and *San Francisco—A City to Remember* and is the author of *Mystique of the Wilderness, Point Reyes—Secret Places & Magic Moments,* and *Yosemite Valley—Secret Places & Magic Moments.* His new book on the Sierra is due to be published in 1995.

Wildcat Beach.